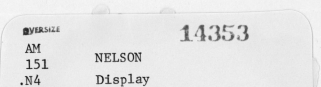

Interiors Library,   3

Display

edited, with an introduction by George Nelson

Interiors Library

published by

Whitney Publications, Inc.

18 East 50 Street

New York 22, N. Y.

53-13449

First Printing 1953
Second Printing 1956

contents

introduction

The word "display" comes from a Latin root which means to unfold or to spread out. As used by us, in a variety of situations, it always conveys the idea of calling someone's attention to something by showing it in a conspicuous way. While the material presented in this book is special in its applications and contemporary in its outlook, it relates nonetheless to an ancient and widely practised art, one which in a sense even antedates the human race. The plumage of the male bird and the antics of the fighting fish are "display." So are the illuminated letters in a medieval manuscript.

The purposes of display are many, although the essential procedures always involve attracting attention. The object of display may be to attract a member of the opposite sex; to establish identity (as in the heraldic symbols blazoned on the shields of the knights, or the markings on the undersides of airplanes); to indicate social position (whether actual or desired) by means of school ties, crowns and tiaras, the amount of land around a house, the uplift in the rear fender of the Cadillac; to convey information, as in road signs, traveling exhibits, posters, billboards. And to attract customers. The great bulk of display, in this unromantic age of ours, is designed to persuade someone to buy something he may or may not need or want.

In a curious, esoteric book by Maurice Collis, *The Land of the Great Image,* the author devotes his considerable talents to descriptions of some forgotten people who lived in unfamiliar places. The time is the 17th Century, and much of the narrative deals with the strange and bloody Portuguese town of Goa, half way up the west coast of India. Goa was a beachhead in the Church's fight to extend its influence into Asia, and its decadent society was ruled by the Inquisition. Hence going to church was an important activity. This is how an upper class lady, "superbly attired in the Portuguese

Mode," went to church: "Her gown is gold brocade, which glows under a mantle of black silk gauze. She comes riding in a palanquin, seated on a Persian carpet and propped on velvet cushions. On foot behind are a score of maid-servants, slave girls from middle or upper India or negroes from Mozambique, bought for their looks and dressed to set them off in colored smocks falling to the navel and wide pleated scarlet petticoats, some carrying a mat, a carpet, a prayer book, others a handkerchief or a fan." And so on. Despite the remoteness of the time, the obscurity of the place and the almost total incomprehensibility of the society, we have no difficulty in identifying this performance as the kind of display it was. The tradition persists and its innumerable expressions can be understood.

The reason for this rather devious introduction to an introduction is that in the book at hand the customary tight lines around the various kinds of display have been somewhat relaxed, and the idea is given a broader meaning than is customary. To some groups of designers and commercial artists, "display" is window display. In other circles it means the moving advertising devices one sees in store windows and railroad waiting rooms. Here it has been taken to cover virtually every three-dimensional design activity in which the main purpose is to show something. Thus, since shops must show their merchandise in order to sell it, examples of shop design are included. Showrooms are in the same category although here the "public" may be a very limited group. Exhibitions, whether world's fairs or small portable shows, have been considered eligible, and they are not segregated according to their purpose. To the designer concerned with the tools and techniques of his trade, it is not of consequence whether a given example has a commercial or educational intent—what counts is the force and clarity with which a communication is established.

Modern work in the many fields of display has a value which goes well beyond its immediate surface meaning. By this I mean that if you are professionally interested in such design activities as shops and exhibitions, this collection of examples, like any other, may be valuable. But if you are not, the value may be even greater. The reason for this apparent paradox lies in the very nature of display: it is temporary. The parade of the Goanese lady and her slaves, the pretty hats in the window, the lacy exhibition buildings at the great fairs—all these are designed to be viewed for a limited time. Occasionally someone miscalculates, as in the case of the Eiffel Tower, erected to serve for a summer at an exposition of 1889 and subsequently adopted as the symbol of a city. The fleeting nature of designs for display has an extraordinary effect on the architect and designer: here, he realizes, he can do his work without the fear that posterity may mock him for his ineptness, and thus freed from the censure of generations unborn he can take a chance, try something out; and, in a word, relax. It is in the relatively relaxed attitude engendered by problems of this kind that one finds the key to so much of its freshness and casual charm and also to its remarkable prophetic nature.

It is an odd thing, but true, that when one begins to trace developments in architecture, structure, interior design and related areas, the old expositions turn out to be remarkably accurate guides to future ways of doing things. Paxton's Crystal Palace, built in 1851, was a prefabricated structure entirely done in metal and glass, and its implications are not fully exhausted a century later. The Hall of Machines, put up for a Paris fair in 1889, set the pace for an entire category of steel structure. Mies van der Rohe became internationally known as an architect with something important to say through two exhibitions; one in 1929, the other in 1931.

In this book you will find a section labeled "systems," and in it have been assembled a considerable number of structures useful for the requirements of interior display. Virtually without exception, these systems build themselves into open cages of steel, wood or aluminum. The advantages of the cages, according to their designers, lies in the flexibility they permit. One can put things in them or on them, open spaces can be filled with solid panels if desired, flooded with light from attached lamps, etc., etc. If these advantages really exist, is it not curious that these solutions hardly existed half a dozen years ago? Why did display structures then consist of panels which could only be assembled into walls and boxes? Obviously the answer does not lie in the functional properties of the new cages, because these could have been established much earlier. What has happened—and this is more of the meaning below the surface mentioned above—is that there has been a change in our feelings about space and how it should be handled. It is not easy to express these feelings in permanent buildings today: there is the conservatism of owners, of building codes, of the FHA, of banks, of trade unions. But in a temporary exposition—why not? The need to be practical doesn't exist, the necessity to build inexpensively does. The designer can ease up a bit and enjoy himself. The result can be fun. It is surprising how often it is significant fun.

George Nelson

11–43

Systems

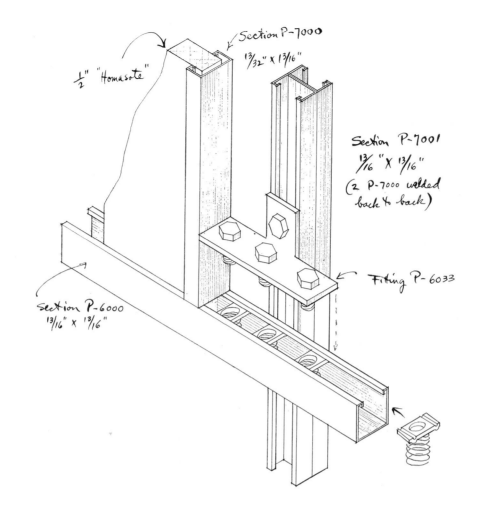

Section P-7000
$13/32" \times 13/16"$

$\frac{1}{2}"$ "Homasote"

Section P-7001
$13/16" \times 13/16"$
(2 P-7000 welded
back to back)

Fitting P-6033

Section P-6000
$13/16" \times 13/16"$

"Unistrut"

John Reider

The Unistrut system was designed by the company's president, Charles W. Attwood, and the original intent was to provide a rack system for power station and industrial use. Since then the virtues of the system—low cost, easy erection and total salvage—have led to its adoption in a wide variety of fields, including exhibition and display. The photographs here show an assembly in the offices of architects: Sanders, Malsin and Reiman, where the framework supports shelves, divided panels, cabinets and lighting fixtures. Unistrut was used with tremendous effectiveness a few years back by Alexander Girard (page 147) in his "For Modern Living" show at the Detroit Institute of Arts. Another installation, by Ray and Charles Eames for the 1950 "Good Design" exhibit, is shown on page 129. The drawing above shows the basic components of the system: rolled sections of various sizes, connectors, bolts and special spring nuts. The only tools required are a wrench for tightening the assemblies and a hacksaw for cutting the sections to length.

continued

Yoshrio Ishmato

Each spring the Institute of Design of the Illinois Institute of Technology holds open
house to show student work and the multiple activities of the school. The exhibition
is always designed as a collaborative project, and is part of the student's work
for the year. The exhibit shown here was done in 1952 by a group of twenty students
under the direction of architects Albert Szabo and Charles Forberg, professors at
the school. The manner in which the Unistrut members have been used is conventional, but it demonstrates in a very clear way some of the many possibilities of
this type of cage structure: there are full-height panels, suspended display boards,
tilted exhibits (top photograph) and combinations of open-mesh and solid backgrounds. One of the great virtues of the cage system is that its parts may be used
again and again while imposing no set design pattern on the resulting display. The
structural members are so thin and inconspicuous, relatively, that they permit the
development of almost any desired character for the display.

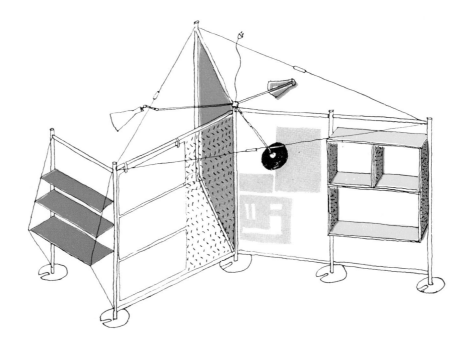

"Struc-Tube"

The Struc-Tube system was designed in 1948 by George Nelson and Associates to answer the need of a greeting card manufacturer for a durable, easily assembled traveling show. Photographs of the exhibit are shown at the right and on the two following pages.

A requirement established by the designers was that the structure be capable of assembly without the use of tools, and the solution was a tubular aluminum framework with keyhole connectors, slip-in base plates and snap fasteners for the hanging panels. Tests using two people unfamiliar with the system showed that the entire exhibit could be uncrated and set up in about ten minutes. The show traveled for about two years and at the end its components were still in good working order.

As the project developed it became apparent that the uses of the system went beyond the limits of the original assignment and a number of other ideas were projected. The sketch above, for instance, showed a small unit which incorporated shelving, various display panels and lighting. Other applications are illustrated in the pages which follow.

Hedrich-Blessing

continued

Below, an overall view of the assembled greeting card exhibit.
All material was mounted on aluminum sheet, an almost ideal material for displays
which get frequent handling. The unit above was not part of the traveling show,
but was set up for a special introductory panel at a museum exhibit.
One of the major advantages of the exhibit structure was provided by
the slotted discs, which gave all the stability needed without bracing,
and greatly facilitated assembly. It was possible for one person
to put the entire exhibit together without assistance.

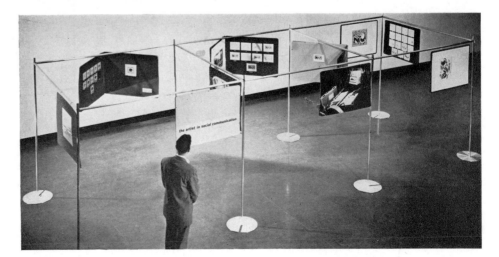

The crate, with directions pasted on, contained all of the components for the traveling exhibition shown on pages 15 and 16. Slots make possible the stacking of bases in the crates.

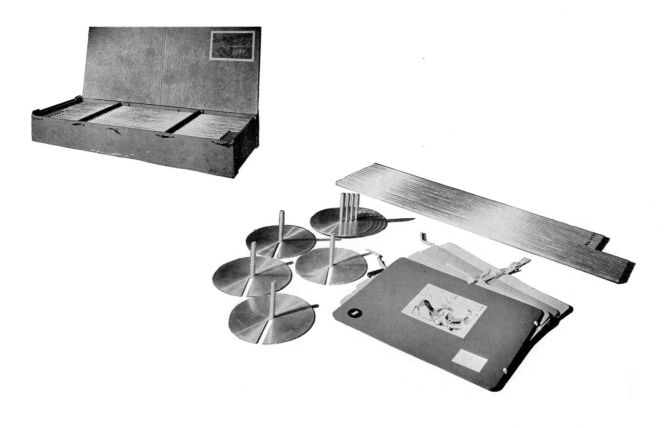

These are the only two connections which were used in the entire exhibition : vertical tube supports which slide on to the bases, and horizontal tubes which lock into the verticals by means of plugs and keyholes.

continued

photos on both pages: Michael

One of the earliest modifications made in the original Struc-Tube system was a device to permit floor-to-ceiling mounting. Three methods were considered: a compression mount using an internal spring, a similar arrangement using a screw, and the solution shown here, which utilizes a telescoping extension which bolts to the ceiling. The lashed canvas screen used for the partition in this anteroom is perfectly satisfactory for situations where visual privacy is all that is required. In cases where quiet is needed as well as partitioning, solid panels acoustically treated could be used. For such installations the standard movable wall systems now on the market would probably be superior in both performance and cost; the virtues of Struc-Tube tend to diminish as demountability becomes less of a factor.

An example of the manner in which accessories can be incorporated into the tube structure. Here a tube has been slotted to accommodate a standard Garcy shelf bracket. In all of the demountable frame systems, provision for the easy attachment of commonly needed accessories is as important as the design of the framework itself.

continued

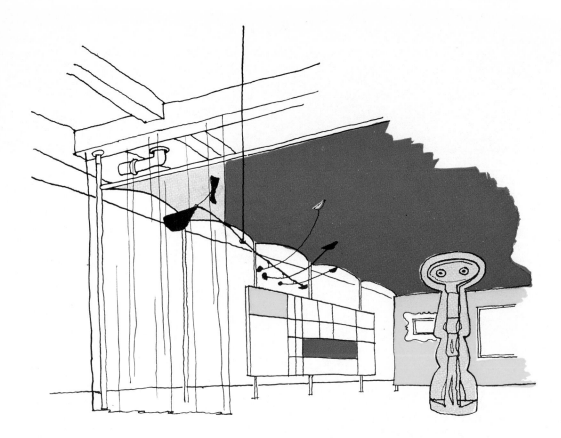

The drawing above envisages the possibility of transforming interiors without structural alterations. Here an exhibit is shown in a loft type of space, with the installation independent of the surrounding walls and ceiling. The temporary ceiling indicated could be made of light sheet materials slightly arched to support themselves between metal angles. Below, a sketch suggesting a possible adaptation of the Struc-Tube frame to use in a department store. The idea was that certain retail requirements might be met with an inventory of components, so that display and storage changes within certain departments might be made with a minimum of disturbance and expense.

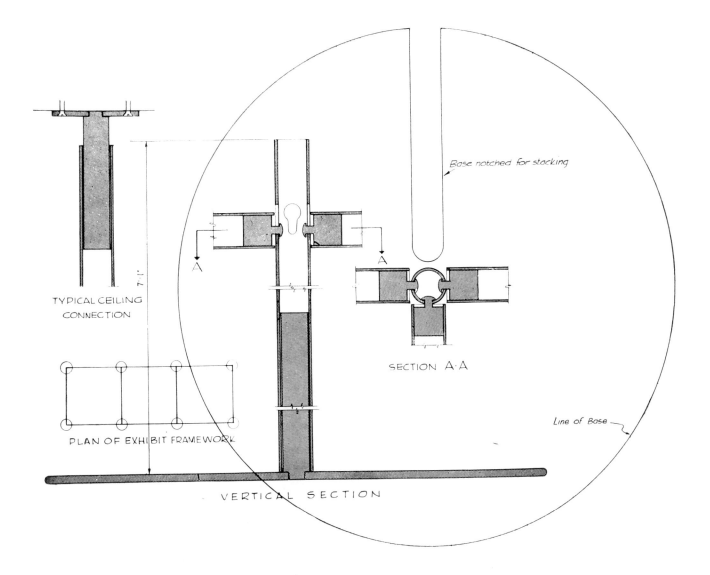

TYPICAL CEILING
CONNECTION

Base notched for stacking

PLAN OF EXHIBIT FRAMEWORK

SECTION A·A

Line of Base

VERTICAL SECTION

Hedrich-Blessing

EMBOSSING

The large circle above represents the slotted base illustrated earlier. Within it are the working parts used in the greeting card exhibit: the vertical tube with its keyhole slots and the horizontal members with plugs machined to fit the keyholes. Also shown outside the circle is a detail of the telescoping ceiling connection which was used on the office partition on page 18. Right: the aluminum placards which represent one of the solutions possible for a traveling show. The placards are attached to the horizontal tubes by plastic straps which attach by means of snap fasteners. One of the main advantages of the plastic straps, aside from their clean appearance and ease of attachment, is the fact that they do not mar the surface of the aluminum tubing. Manufacturer of the Struc-Tube system is the Affiliated Machine & Tool Co.

continued

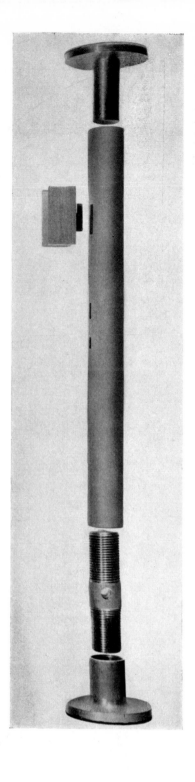

A number of modifications later built into the Struc-Tube framing system are shown here. Rubber-surfaced floor and ceiling plates, and a screw insert permit erection without the need for fasteners. A slotted connection (left) permits the incorporation of solid panels. The drawing below shows another type of connector: multi-pronged aluminum castings whose ends fit into the tubes and create a fairly rigid framework where connection to the ceiling is impossible or undesirable.

One of the most handsome of the installations ever made with the Struc-Tube frame-work is this interior in the Fine Arts Center at the University of Arkansas, a brilliantly successful building designed by Edward D. Stone Associates. The system is used in the large exhibition hall with the tubes extending from floor to ceiling. Each of the panels, which serves both as a display background and a space divider, is supported by its own pair of uprights. This duplication of vertical members was not envisaged in the original system, but it has the advantage that each section of the display can be handled independently.

The lighting of the space is also worth noting for it matches the display system in flexibility. It was also developed by the Nelson office. The idea of exposed wiring, to which fixtures might be attached anywhere along the length of the conduit, is not a new one. It had been used for years in factories, particularly where assembly line work made it necessary to have mobile electrical connections to permit workers to move portable lamps along the line. The wiring duct is fitted with specially designed clamp-on bullets which can be shifted with no more equipment than a ladder.

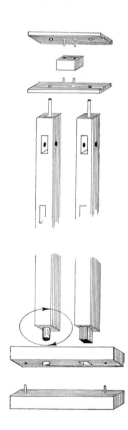

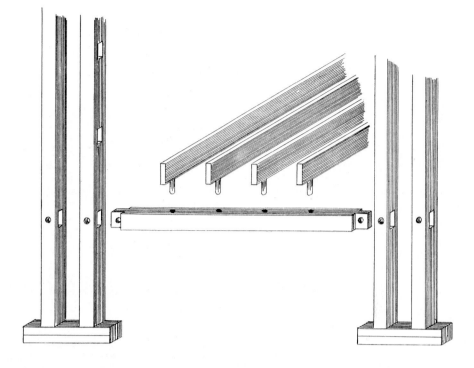

"H"-System

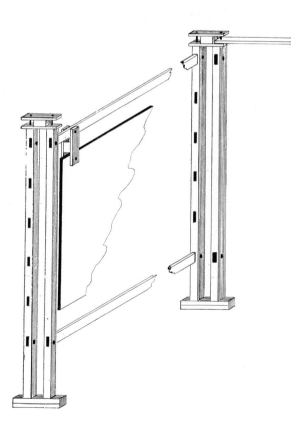

To develop an exhibit system in wood which is completely demountable and simple to assemble is more difficult than in metal; but, as
this example shows, it is entirely possible. The framework is fabri-
cated in clear pine and the connections consist of the traditional pegs,
dowels, mortises and tenons. The standard package consists of 160
pieces and includes uprights, stretcher beams, base blocks, H-fittings
(to hold panels and other inserts), louver wings and panels. Uprights
are 7'-5" high; stretchers and panels, a variety of sizes. The whole
package is shipped in three boxes. Photographs indicate something
of the variety of arrangements possible with this package, and the
drawings clearly show the components involved and the system for
their assembly. Inevitably a framework of this construction lacks
the delicacy of a comparable one in metal, but the sturdiness of the
system, its direct expression of the material, its simplicity and
flexibility entitle it to consideration on its own merits. This "H"
system and others are recorded in a catalog available from the
designer-manufacturer: Martin Metal & Associates.

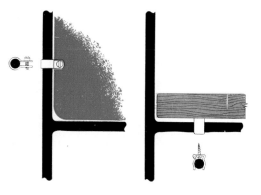

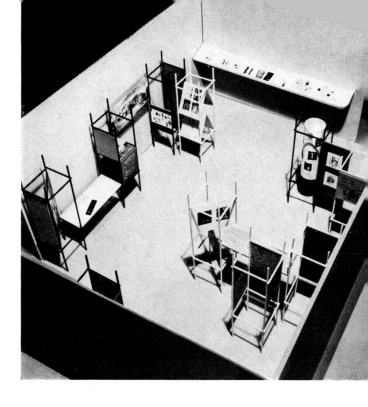

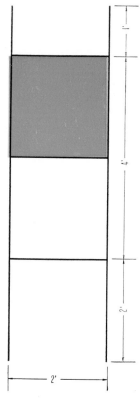

Traveling Exhibit

An exceedingly elegant display by Alvin Lustig, designed to show his own work in graphic design, interior and frabics. The core of the exhibit consists of ten cages of 5/16″ steel rod, welded as shown. Five are painted black and five are white, and dimensions of the different units are varied sufficiently so that they can be nested for shipping. The slight differences in size which make the nesting possible are not noticeable when the cages are set up in the exhibit. Lustig, who has established a secure place for himself as one of the top U. S. graphic designers, worked out his show so that the exhibits were what counted. The cages are sufficiently delicate in scale so that they do not detract from the panels they hold.

Two types of clips, shown in the drawings, are used to hold the panels to the rods: thin mounting sheets are bolted through to clips already attached to the rods; heavier panels have clips screwed in and these are snapped on to the rods. The show has been seen in the A.D. Gallery in New York, the Frank Perls Gallery in Los Angeles, as well as a number of museums and universities.

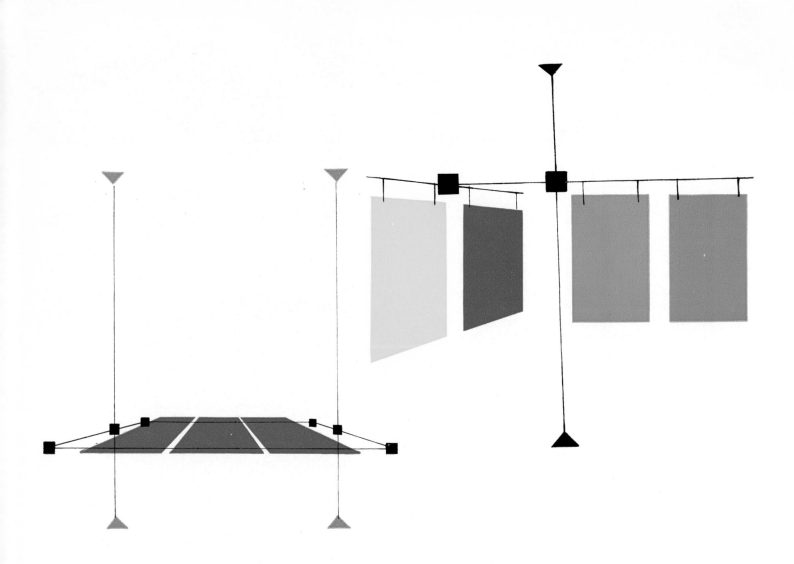

Horizontals can be fitted between verticals, supported from a central pole, or arranged to make a horizontal display. The rubber suction discs cling to uneven floors or ceilings, and make possible the use of an unsympathetic setting, such as a staircase (facing page). There is no limit to the vertical height of the poles which are built on a 6-foot module, but eleven feet is the limit of a horizontal supported on one end only. Leather straps and United-Carr snap fasteners hold the flat panels to the horizontals.

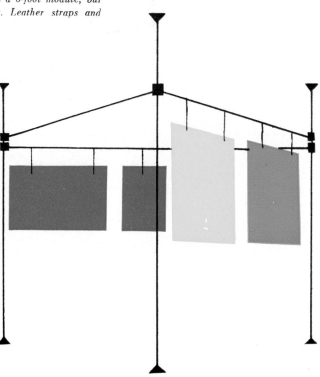

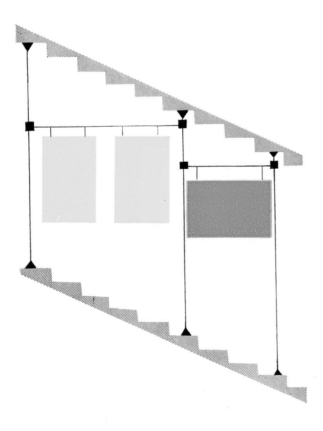

"Flexible Display"

The background of this display system is interesting—
it was designed as a senior thesis by Joseph Carreiro,
William Daley and Charles Quillin while they were
students at the Massachusetts School of Art. The team
took as its problem a package of portable display units
with such desirable characteristics as adaptability, lightness, compactness, low cost and ease of assembly. The
solution, appropriately developed as a full-scale exhibition for the school, shows all of these qualities plus a
very handsome appearance. The connector blocks re-
semble both the fittings for metal scaffolding and for
laboratory apparatus, but they have their own logic in
this application and are entirely appropriate as used.
The spring-loaded posts are completely workable, and
they represent an economical solution as well.

Pine & Baker, for whom Joseph Carreiro has designed
furniture, is considering the manufacture of the system.

continued

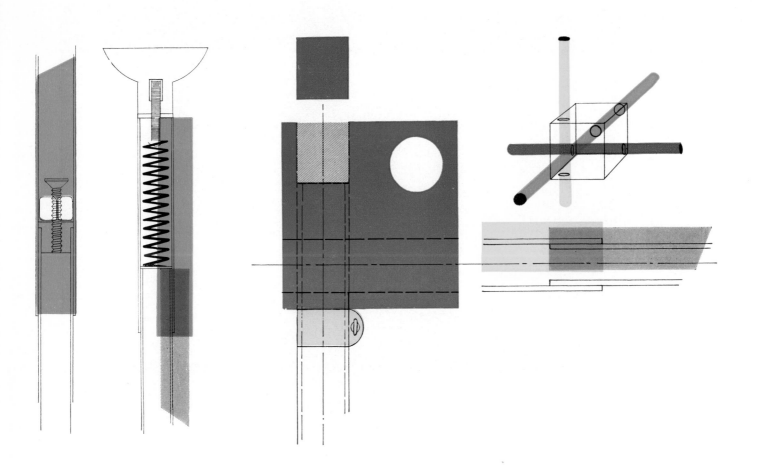

Above, drawings of the spring unit which provides the adjustability of the rod lengths; the cam and bushing and connectors. Right, these exhibition elements shown as they are assembled in specially designed boxes (the method for packing and shipping was considered an integral part of the project), and the standard panels for Flexible Display which are slotted for lightness and fastening convenience.

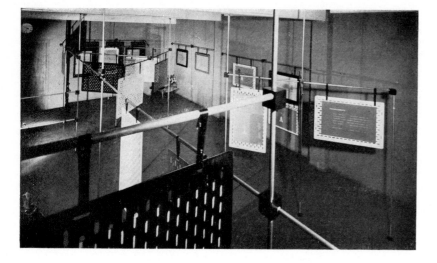

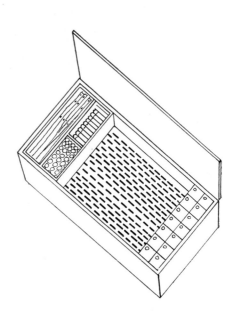

Assembly with Tubes and Clamps

"The New Landscape", at the Charles Hayden Memorial Library, Massachusetts Institute of Technology (1951). Gyorgy Kepes, designer; Thomas McNulty, assistant.

Ever since the idea of the cage structure took hold with designers, there has been (as the material in this section amply demonstrates) a constant search for new ways of making the structures. Since the "making" of a structure is entirely a matter of connectors, it is around the problem of the joints that all design research has revolved. In this exhibit by Gyorgy Kepes, the research was boiled down to the location of a firm manufacturing the standard three-way connectors used in chemistry laboratories. As used here, the structure forms a delicate, neutral and wonderfully appropriate adjunct to the display material. So sparingly has the cage been handled that many of the mounted photographs are supported, not by the tubes, but by thin, almost invisible wires.

The theme of the exhibit is "The New Landscape"—title of a forthcoming book by Kepes, to be published by the Technology Press in Cambridge. The material of both book and exhibition is the world as seen through the instruments of scientific and technological research: the telescopes, high-speed cameras, electron microscopes and innumerable other devices for exploration and measurement. The highly "abstract" nature of this emerging world is suggested by the exhibits visible in the illustrations, shapes and patterns of a remarkable and unfamiliar richness. It is possible that as these glimpses of the contemporary scene become more familiar, the activities of modern artists, particularly the painters, will come to seem less mysterious.

The small photographs show some of the combinations produced by the stand-ard components. One of the most interesting is the development of a second level. On these high panels some of the larger paintings are displayed: their most valuable function, however, is the screening of the interior architecture of whatever space the show is set up in. Requirements of the exhibit include only the provision of a minimum ceiling height and floor area. Lighting is provided by whatever units exist in the room used for the show.

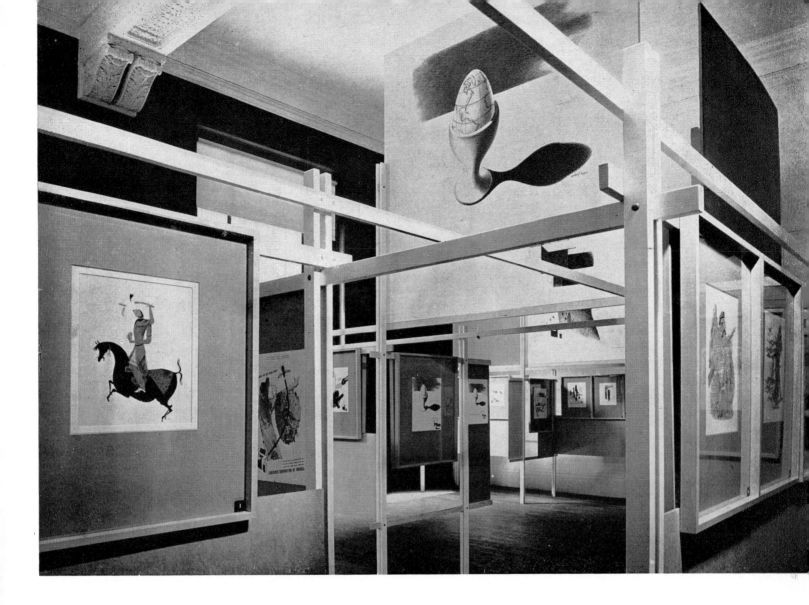

Demountable Exhibit

The remarkably enlightened position taken by the Container Corporation of America in matters where design is a factor is perhaps best known to readers of those magazines in which its advertisements have appeared. These graphic productions have used artists in numbers probably unmatched by any other U. S. Commercial enterprise, and it was to indicate the scope of this project that the traveling exhibition shown here was designed. The problems presented were the standard problems: a framework easily put up and taken down, units of standard sizes to fit into crates, a structural arrangement which is self-sufficient so that no demands are made on surrounding walls, floors or ceilings. The approach used here is a system of pre-drilled wood uprights which are integrated with matching horizontal members and finished panels. The design differs from many of the other cage structures illustrated, in that here the frame is sufficiently conspicuous to form an important design element in itself. Use of wood members of generous dimensions also serves to mark off the separate items of the exhibit which consists entirely of pictures. Designer: Herbert Bayer; collaborator, Stamo Papadaki.

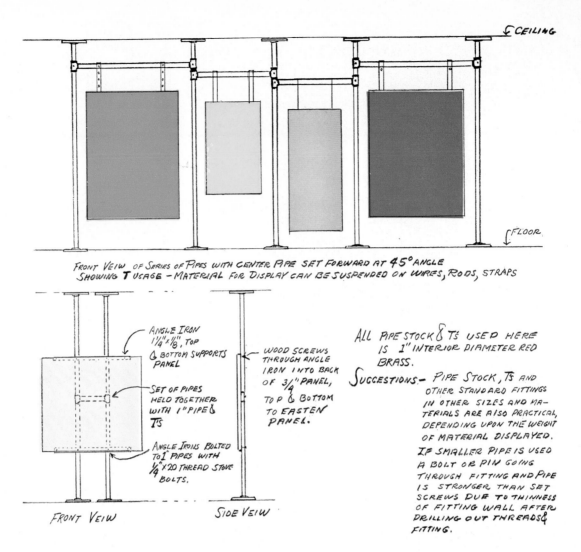

FRONT VEIW OF SERIES OF PIPES WITH CENTER PIPE SET FORWARD AT 45° ANGLE
SHOWING T USAGE - MATERIAL FOR DISPLAY CAN BE SUSPENDED ON WIRES, RODS, STRAPS

ANGLE IRON
1¼"x⅛", TOP
& BOTTOM SUPPORTS
PANEL

SET OF PIPES
HELD TOGETHER
WITH 1" PIPE &
T'S

ANGLE IRONS BOLTED
TO 1" PIPES WITH
¼"x20 THREAD STOVE
BOLTS.

WOOD SCREWS
THROUGH ANGLE
IRON INTO BACK
OF ¾" PANEL,
TOP & BOTTOM
TO EASTEN
PANEL.

FRONT VEIW   SIDE VEIW

ALL PIPE STOCK & T'S USED HERE
IS 1" INTERIOR DIAMETER RED
BRASS.
SUGGESTIONS.- PIPE STOCK, T'S AND
OTHER STANDARD FITTINGS
IN OTHER SIZES AND MA-
TERIALS ARE ALSO PRACTICAL,
DEPENDING UPON THE WEIGHT
OF MATERIAL DISPLAYED.
IF SMALLER PIPE IS USED
A BOLT OR PIN GOING
THROUGH FITTING AND PIPE
IS STRONGER THAN SET
SCREWS DUE TO THINNESS
OF FITTING WALL AFTER
DRILLING OUT THREADS &
FITTING.

Plumbers' Pipes

Most of the display structures shown in this book share a common point of origin—the designer was presented with a specific exhibit problem, with ease of erection and demounting as one of the requirements—and in the course of working out his solution found that he had developed a system. Here is what is perhaps the least "designed" of these systems since it depends entirely on plumbing pipes and connections. It too developed out of a specific situation. The mosaicist Jeanne Reynal had been having difficulty in setting up her exhibitions because of her desire to have her compositions regarded as paintings in stone rather than conventional mosaics. Since mosaics take on, as a rule, the character of walls, it was desired in this case to display them free of gallery walls so that there could be no confusion regarding the artist's intention. A last-minute solution worked out by a fellow artist, Urban Neininger, involved the purchase of lengths of brass pipe and fittings, and the use of plywood and sponge rubber discs where the pipes had to extend from floor to ceiling. Like all such impromptu solutions the result has a simple logic and a straightforward appearace. However, it also lacks some of the convenience of the exhibit systems in which more thought has been given to problems of assembly and removal.

Ben Schnall

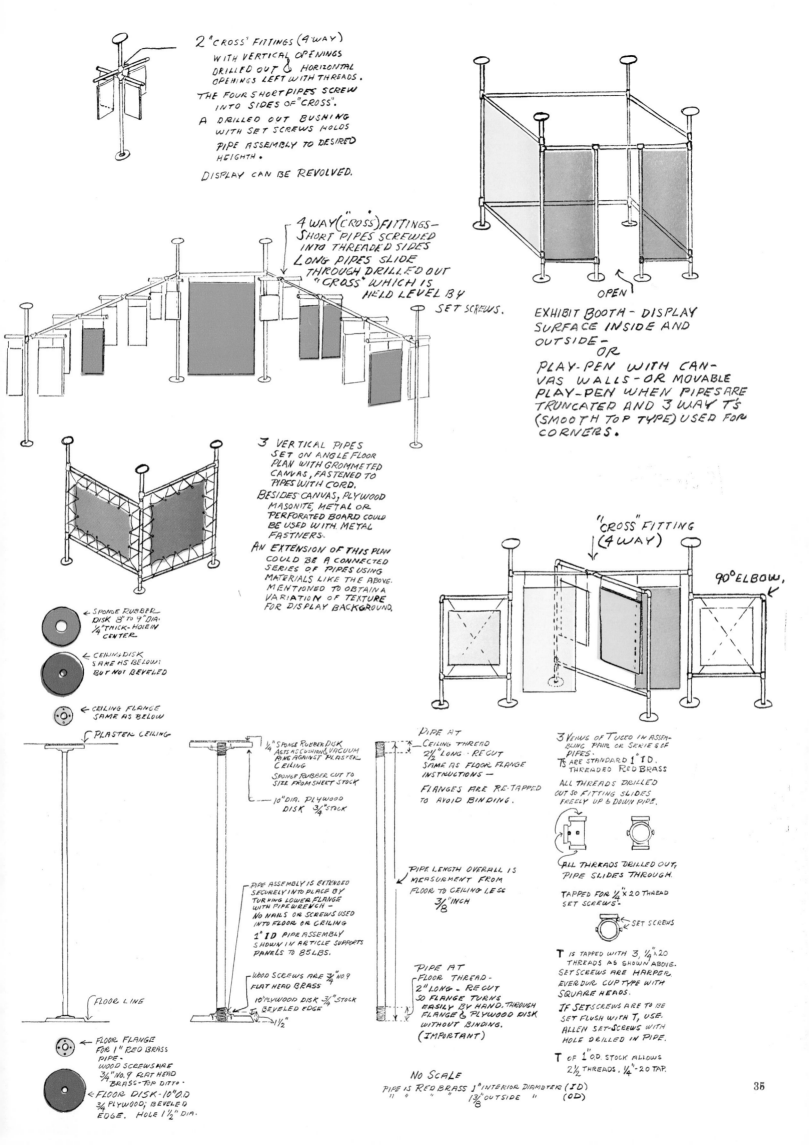

2 "CROSS" FITTINGS (4 WAY) WITH VERTICAL OPENINGS DRILLED OUT & HORIZONTAL OPENINGS LEFT WITH THREADS.

THE FOUR SHORT PIPES SCREW INTO SIDES OF "CROSS".

A DRILLED OUT BUSHING WITH SET SCREWS HOLDS PIPE ASSEMBLY TO DESIRED HEIGHT.

DISPLAY CAN BE REVOLVED.

4 WAY ("CROSS") FITTINGS - SHORT PIPES SCREWED INTO THREADED SIDES LONG PIPES SLIDE THROUGH DRILLED OUT "CROSS" WHICH IS HELD LEVEL BY SET SCREWS.

OPEN

EXHIBIT BOOTH - DISPLAY SURFACE INSIDE AND OUTSIDE - OR PLAY-PEN WITH CANVAS WALLS - OR MOVABLE PLAY-PEN WHEN PIPES ARE TRUNCATED AND 3 WAY T'S (SMOOTH TOP TYPE) USED FOR CORNERS.

3 VERTICAL PIPES SET ON ANGLE FLOOR PLAN WITH GROMMETED CANVAS, FASTENED TO PIPES WITH CORD.

BESIDES CANVAS, PLYWOOD MASONITE, METAL OR PERFORATED BOARD COULD BE USED WITH METAL FASTNERS.

AN EXTENSION OF THIS PLAN COULD BE A CONNECTED SERIES OF PIPES USING MATERIALS LIKE THE ABOVE MENTIONED TO OBTAIN A VARIATION OF TEXTURE FOR DISPLAY BACKGROUND.

"CROSS" FITTING (4 WAY)

90° ELBOW

← SPONGE RUBBER DISK 8" to 9" DIA. ¼" THICK - HOLE IN CENTER

← CEILING DISK SAME AS BELOW: BUT NOT BEVELED

← CEILING FLANGE SAME AS BELOW

PLASTER CEILING

¼" SPONGE RUBBER DISK ACTS AS CUSHION & VACUUM RING AGAINST PLASTER CEILING

SPONGE RUBBER CUT TO SIZE FROM SHEET STOCK

10" DIA. PLYWOOD DISK ¾" STOCK

PIPE AT CEILING THREAD 2½" LONG - RE CUT SAME AS FLOOR FLANGE INSTRUCTIONS -

FLANGES ARE RE-TAPPED TO AVOID BINDING.

3 VIEWS OF T USED IN ASSEMBLING PAIR OR SERIES OF PIPES. T'S ARE STANDARD 1" ID THREADED RED BRASS

ALL THREADS DRILLED OUT SO FITTING SLIDES FREELY UP & DOWN PIPE.

ALL THREADS DRILLED OUT, PIPE SLIDES THROUGH.

TAPPED FOR ¼" X 20 THREAD SET SCREWS.

← SET SCREWS

T IS TAPPED WITH 3, ¼" X 20 THREADS AS SHOWN ABOVE. SET SCREWS ARE HARPER EVERDUR CUP TYPE WITH SQUARE HEADS.

IF SET SCREWS ARE TO BE SET FLUSH WITH T, USE ALLEN SET-SCREWS WITH HOLE DRILLED IN PIPE.

T OF 1" O.D. STOCK ALLOWS 2½ THREADS. ¼"-20 TAP.

PIPE ASSEMBLY IS EXTENDED SECURELY INTO PLACE BY TURNING LOWER FLANGE WITH PIPE WRENCH - NO NAILS OR SCREWS USED INTO FLOOR OR CEILING

1" ID PIPE ASSEMBLY SHOWN IN ARTICLE SUPPORTS PANELS TO 85 LBS.

WOOD SCREWS ARE ¾" NO.9 FLAT HEAD BRASS 10" PLYWOOD DISK ¾" STOCK BEVELED EDGE.

1½"

PIPE LENGTH OVERALL IS MEASURMENT FROM FLOOR TO CEILING LESS ⅜ "INCH

PIPE AT FLOOR THREAD - 2" LONG - RE CUT SO FLANGE TURNS EASILY BY HAND THROUGH FLANGE & PLYWOOD DISK WITHOUT BINDING. (IMPORTANT)

FLOOR LINE

← FLOOR FLANGE FOR 1" RED BRASS PIPE. WOOD SCREWS ARE ¾" NO.9 FLAT HEAD BRASS - TOP DITTO.

← FLOOR DISK - 10" O.D. ¾ PLYWOOD; BEVELED EDGE. HOLE 1½" DIA.

NO SCALE
PIPE IS RED BRASS 1" INTERIOR DIAMETER (ID)
"   "   "   1⅜" OUTSIDE "   (OD)

35

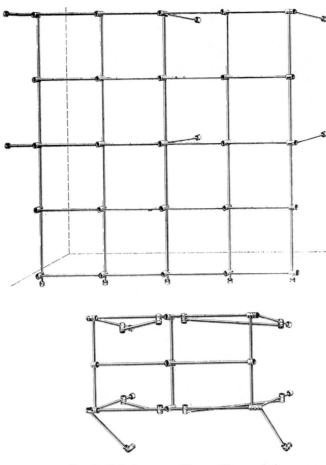

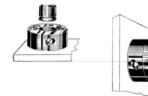

*Two Emil Greiner assemblies are illustrated above.
The light, strong, aluminum alloy pipes are solid,
but hollow tubes are also available. A versatile
Universal Clamp, which can be threaded in two
directions at right angles, is one of the system's basic
features. A floor and a wall clamp are illustrated below.*

Laboratory Frames

Demountable exhibit structures show a strong resemblance, in most cases, to demountable structures developed for other purposes. This is perfectly natural, since there is a limit to the number of kinds and types of connectors which can be devised, and it is the connectors which establish the character, appearance and utility of the system. Illustrated here are two commercially produced systems offered for use in laboratories: their applicability to display is quite obvious, and the types of connectors employed are therefore interesting. The Greiner assemblies, shown above, use tubes of aluminum alloy and a kind of universal clamp which can be fitted in two directions at right angles. The Fisher Flexiframe system is also made in aluminum, and it too has connectors which permit great freedom in setting up assemblies. Both offer all sorts of accessories including pieces which permit permanent fastening to walls or floors. The handsome, workmanlike appearance of parts and assemblies is typical of much equipment produced for laboratory and industrial use. The similarity of these frames, not only to exhibit structures illustrated elsewhere in the book, but to the immortal Tinker Toy, will not escape the reader.

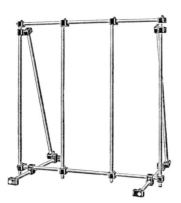

The Fischer Company's Flexaframe assemblies, made of an aluminum alloy called Castaloy, are similar to Greiner's. Components are sold individually—rods, connectors, and clamps. Frames can be screwed to wall, floor or ceiling, or stand free.

Rectangular Flexaframe clamp doubles as a floor balance, similar to the Greiner system. There are also innumerable clamps for holding flasks, rods, rubber tubes. Diagram at left shows the rigid support connections attainable with two Flexaframe connectors and a 1⅝″ rod.

Flexaframe rods are half an inch in diameter, and come in lengths from 1⅝″ to 72″.

The Flexaframe foot is used for permanent assemblies. Each has 3 countersunk screw holes and a ground central hole to receive a Flexaframe rod. A slotted square head setscrew locks the rod in position.

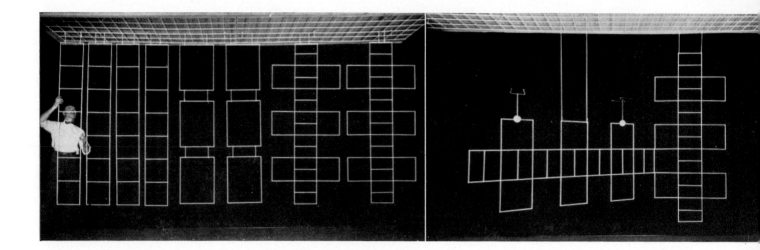

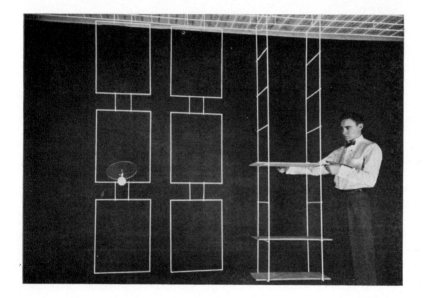

Top photo shows the various elements hung from the ceiling grid. Right, a "ladder" is used for shelving; and below, a slotted ball supports a glass shelf.

"Seelingrill"

The "Seelingrill" differs from all of the other systems shown here in that it depends on the ceiling rather than the floor for support. It was devised to help window display designers to float displays from above, making maximum use of horizontal space without cluttering the floor. Basic component of the system is a welded grill of steel bars set in six-inch squares, and it is available in 3' x 6' and 4' x 8' sections. A variety of "ladders" and other vertical elements are available, and components of the system are sold in any desired combination or quantity. The illustrations make it abundantly clear that an enormous variety of installations can be worked out with these elements. Designer-manufacturer is the Bliss Display Corporation.

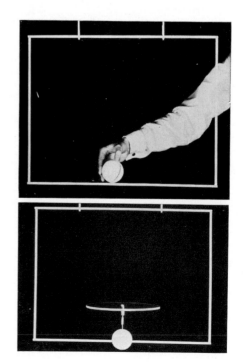

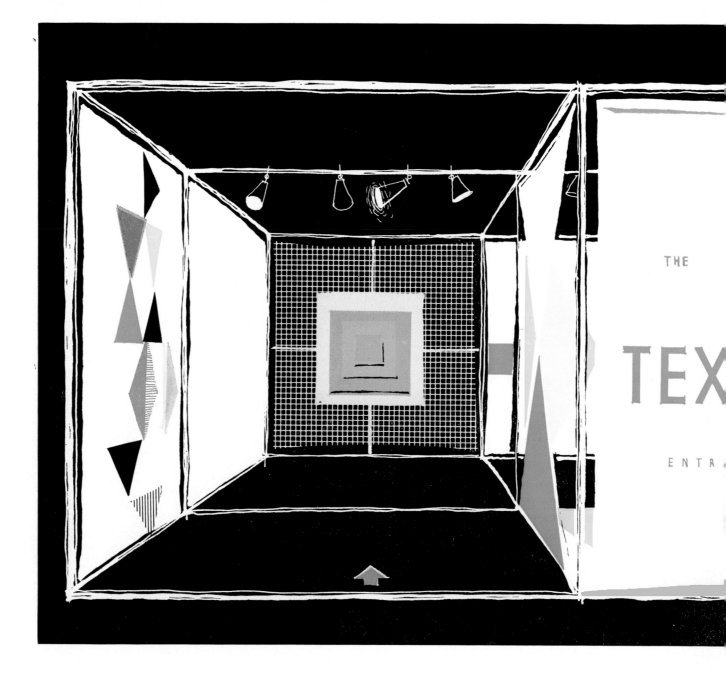

Exhibition Structure

Possibly the most difficult of all display problems is the traveling exhibit which must be set up and taken down at each new place by people completely unfamiliar with it. It has to be simple, rugged, protected from misuse Insurance against the loss of fastening tools and vital small parts has somehow to be built into the design. This is one reason the majority of traveling shows consist of placards which require only wall fastening. The fabric exhibition shown here was produced for the Smithsonian Institute as part of a series prepared for circulation in Europe. Purpose of the displays is to show examples of U. S. design and production. The exhibit illustrated here is a brilliant solution to a complicated set of problems. In it the enclosure, dividers and display material are all one, thus eliminating the usual split between exhibits and backgrounds. Utilization of the bracing wires as fabric supports further integrates the design and creates an unexpectedly dramatic effect. The show is entirely independent of its surroundings—set up in any space large enough to hold it, it provides its own exterior and interior. Designer: Florence Knoll and the Planning Unit of Kroll Associates.

continued

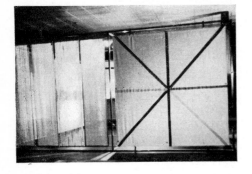

photos: Alexandre Georges

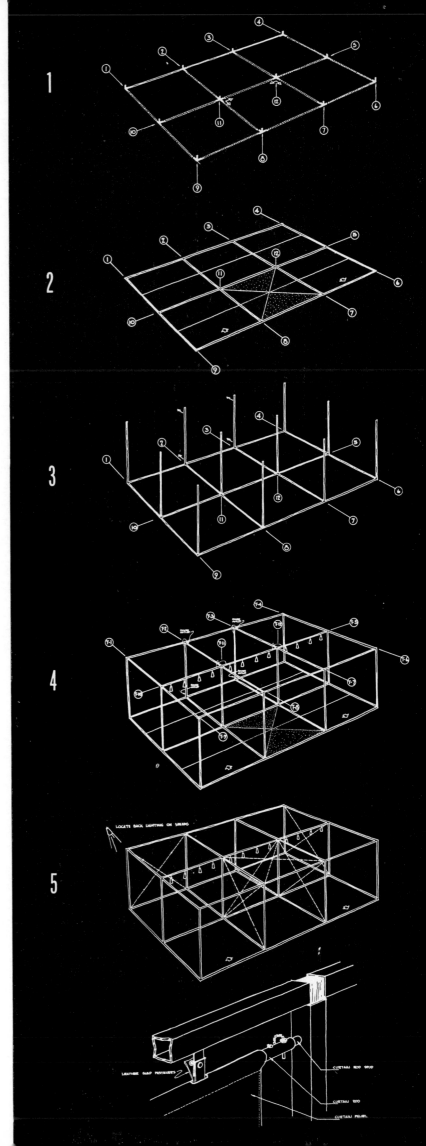

The textile exhibition structure, as it is taken out of the crates, leaves no margin for error. Members are numbered and assembled in a stipulated order, as shown at right. The floor grid, composed of 17 8-foot aluminum tubes, is laid first (1), connected by the patented joint found in some Knoll furniture pieces. Black linoleum floor panels are then set in place (2), vertical tubes rise (3), and the ceiling grid is laid on (4). Electrical jumper cords at points T-2, T-3, T-11 and T-12 hook up to the current in two series of six lamps each. The directions of the spotlights are fixed to light the show as the Knoll Planning Unit specified. Guy wires hooked to the vertical beams (5) provide the frames for the triangular pieces. Then the curtain rods attached to each textile are inserted in holes near the tops of vertical beams and the fabric unrolled. The rods are secured with locking pins, and leather fasteners are snapped to hold the textiles in place.

"Para-sol"

In every field of creative activity "impractical" suggestions have an important role to play. As solutions not susceptible to development with conventional methods, they tend to expand the scope of the assumed problem, free the imagination and to generate other ideas more immediately usable. In their sketches for a vast display hall which they have named "Para-Sol," designers Warren Nardin and Albert Radoczy propose a building which rests on a single central support. Like the Japanese bamboo and paper parasol from which the design takes both idea and name, it consists of a shaft, struts, cantilevered ribs and a fabric top which goes into tenison when the struts are in position. From the engineering point of view the structure can be criticized: wind loads would present staggering problems, the steel ribs would not function as shown, and so on. But this is not quite the point.

The idea is another attack on the problem of the exhibition hall, so frequently set up with a confusion of columns. The object here is to create a new kind of unobstructed space, extremely light in weight, and somewhere between temporary and permanent in its character. As such, it focusses attention on problems which exist and suggests even more strongly some technological gaps yet to be filled. One of the most useful types of materials still to appear would be a light-diffusing sheet, much higher in tensile strength than canvas and less subject to rapid deterioration, proof against the action of both moisture and ultra-violet, and light in weight. As such materials tend to appear, designers and architects will be able to get closer to their goals of more space and more light.

continued

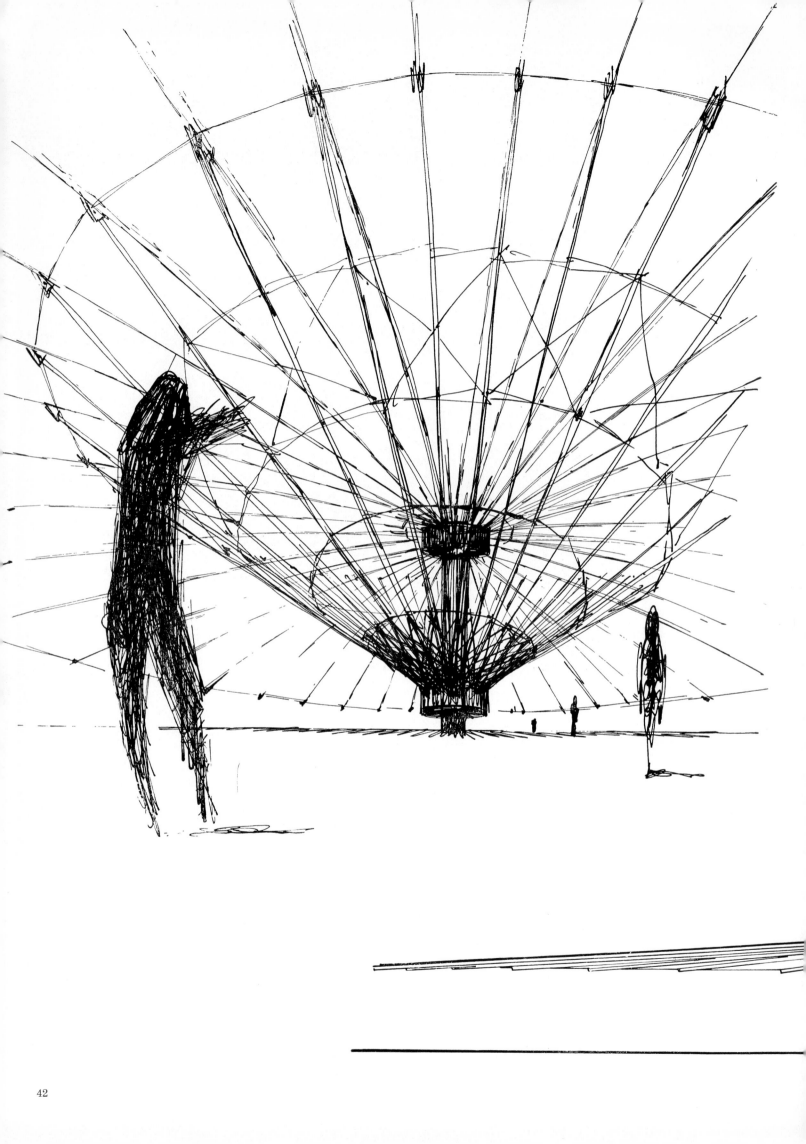

Giant "Para-sol" of steel would have a concrete handle and a canvas cover. The fanning rib-work would be braced against a central steel mast embedded in the concrete column. A hanging outside wall of canvas or stiff sheeting could convert the "Para-sol" into a tent or an enclosed building.

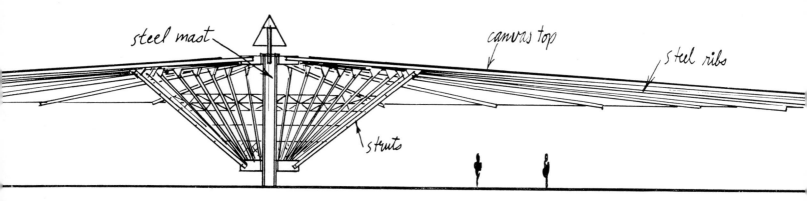

steel mast

canvas top

steel ribs

struts

45-106

Displays

Fabrics at Laverne are hung as they would be for curtains. Elsewhere in the showroom, heavier material in bolts is kept on accessible shelves. Responsible for the interior is a team of designers: Ross Littell, William Katavolos and Douglas Kelley who also design furniture for the firm as well as some fabrics and wallpapers.

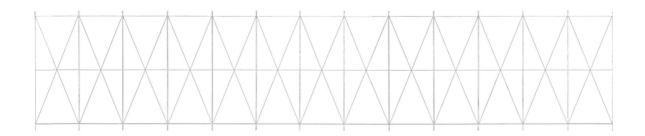

photos: Alexandre Georges

One problem with which manufacturers in the home furnishings field are constantly plagued is the necessity of constant redesign and refurbishing of their showrooms. In the past few years the normal competitive situation has been greatly intensified by rapid shifts in taste and styles, and as a result almost any showroom gets to look old within a very short space of time. This situation has been particularly noticeable in the showrooms devoted to the display of contemporary designs for the extreme emphasis on achieving the latest in exhibit techniques is in itself a factor in promoting faster obsolescence.

The museum-like interior of the showroom of Laverne Originals shows one workable scheme for getting out of this dilemma. The space is treated as if it were a kind of glorified warehouse in which exhibits can be placed—like stacked crates—in any desired relation to each other. Such an interior can be wide open and uncluttered, as shown, packed tight with displays, made dark or light, colorful or quiet. It is a scheme designed, in other words, to cope with the widest possible range of future contingencies.

A scheme of this type can be compared quite appropriately to a stage set. It has the same flexibility and the same possibilities for shifts in dramatic emphasis. Its "props" are the merchandise displays, the visible storage units, the furniture and decorative accessories. This type of approach is beyond a doubt due for more and more attention, for it meets the problem of interior alteration with greater economy than any other.

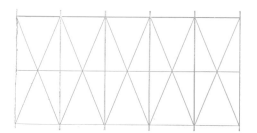

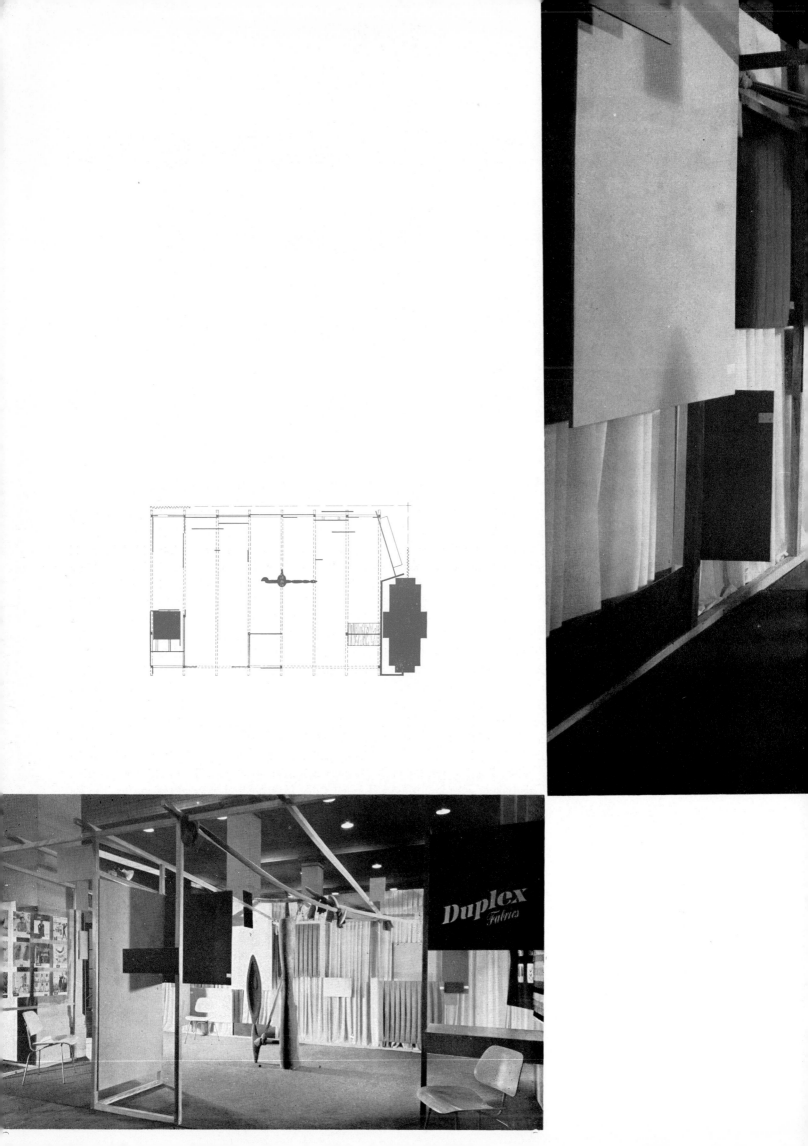

Anyone who has ever participated as a designer in any of the trade shows held in the huge barn-like structures usually set aside for this purpose knows how many headaches are concealed in the seemingly simple problem of designing an effective display booth. Worst of these difficulties stems from the impossibility of anticipating the nature of the adjoining exhibits. Eliminating distractions created by the room itself is also a problem, and many trade exhibits have rules prohibiting the erection of ceilings and wall-height dividers. Considered in the light of these stumbling blocks, this display by Warren Nardin and Albert Radoczy is admirable. It reduces outside interference to a practical minimum and is still sufficiently visible to attract the attention of any passer-by. From a cost point of view, the solution is also worth looking at: aside from the sculpture by Radoczy which serves as a visual center, there is little except a light structure of poles and fabric panels, and the effect created is all out of proportion to the apparent cost.

Two small display units from the textile section of the 1951 Triennale in Milan, designed by Tedeschi, Ponti and Mariani. The upper illustration shows a design to call attention to a dress fabric—the faceless mannequin in a glass case set above floor level allows no uncertainty about what is the main object of display. A different idea is developed in the lower unit, but the result—focus on the display to the exclusion of everything else—is the same. While exceedingly modest as display devices, both units indicate very clearly the highly developed skill of contemporary Italian designers in handling problems of this kind.

The fabric section of the New York showroom of Knoll Associates can be taken as a model of its kind. The simplicity of the scheme suggested in the photograph is deceptive—even casual study of this small area reveals a very carefully calculated effect and an exceedingly workmanlike disposition of the elements. The fabrics themselves are grouped to form walls, strongly lighted and in brilliant color. As a partial screen for the space, and as a way of hiding an unwanted column, Herbert Matter has set up a photographic panel showing parts of old French looms. Between this panel and the white screen on the other side of the column, there are closely spaced shelves which neatly accommodate small fabric samples. Not part of the fabric display, but interesting as an unusually effective display device, is the pool which appears in the foreground. A shallow pan set on the showroom floor, this small plant-filled pool serves as a low area divider and adds greatly to the charm and luxury of this distinguished interior. Designer: Florence Knoll.

Damora

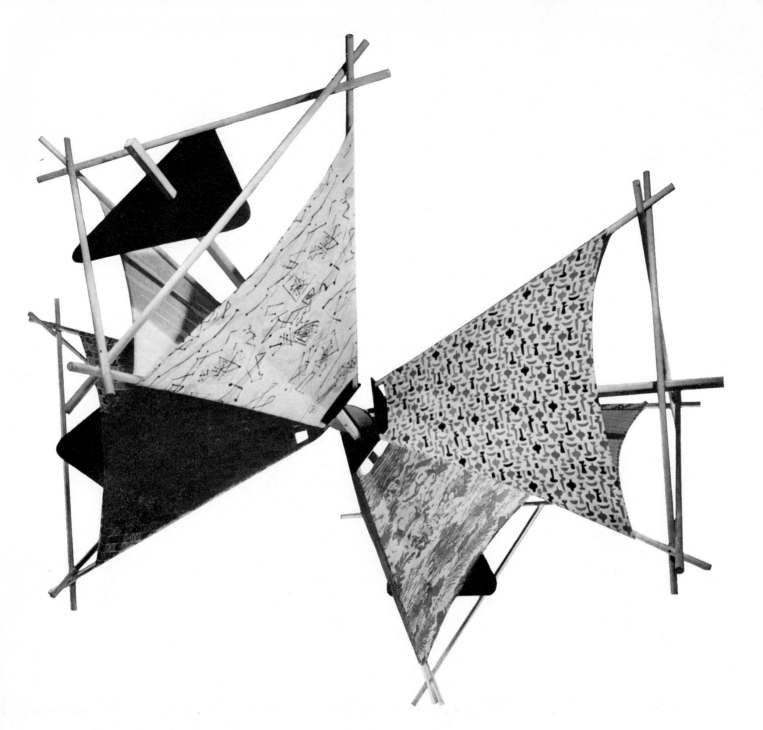

Thomas Yee

The fabric display shown here was set up as a five-day exhibit for Schiffer Prints, illustrating print designs by Wormley, Eames, Dali, Sorensen, Nelson and Rudofsky. The space was a high-ceilinged room in a rather shabby state, and the solution adopted by the designer was the creation of a "forest" of hanging fabrics which took attention away from the walls and made use of the room's height. The kite-like affair was a large construction of fabric-covered poles, hung in the center of the space opposite the entrance. Spectacular in size and shape, it served as the visual focus and effectively stated the theme. Designer: George Nelson and Associates.

photos: Evelyn Hofer

Two views of a former showroom of D. D. and Leslie Tillett, designers and makers of printed textiles. The design vocabulary of the showroom is simple in the extreme: iron rod is the single display element, and it has been used for both the freestanding showcase and the wall exhibits. Doris D. Tillett, designer.

It is only rarely that the design of a showroom sets a theme which is so consistently repeated throughout the space that a unity is created over and above the consistency provided by the merchandise itself. There is also the problem, in showroom design, of the relative importance of the background. It is possible to create interiors for display in which the background is "invisible," so to speak, and it is equally possible to take the opposite approach. Occasionally the product gives the clue to the solution, but equally often it is the personal preference of the designer.

Here, in the showroom for Covington Fabrics, a theme has been established very strongly and directly by the use of textures of solids and voids. All wall textures are produced by wood slats of varying width and spacing. The ceiling is a metal mesh which covers the usual confusion of pipes, beams, ducts and sprinklers. The result is a series of highly visible backgrounds which accent the product—printed cotton fabrics—in a rather striking way. Use of the textured backgrounds had another value in this installation: the color combinations used in the printed fabrics vary enormously and the display problem would be quite complicated if color backgrounds were used. With this solution the base colors are gray and natural wood only, and the prints can therefore be used to give the showroom any color which might be desired. Another virtue of the scheme is that hanging of the fabrics presents no problem. Designers: Katz, Waisman, Blumenkrantz, Stein and Weber (Architects Associated). Displays by Nardin, Radoczy and Mayen.

Left, a detail of one of the main walls. Use of the wood slat pattern in two directions improves the display background and increases possibilities for attachment of fabrics.

Bins for storage of samples and the display easels were specially designed. Cabinets and easel form a three-piece unit which folds on itself when not in use.

Ben Schnall

Batteries of pivoted display panels give the New York showroom of J. H. Thorp & Company something of the look of a large office filled with uniform filing cabinets. In this scheme focal exhibits count for very little. The workmanlike atmosphere is not at all unpleasant, and it reflects the large line of patterns and the big volume of business transacted. Designer: Lester C. Tichy.

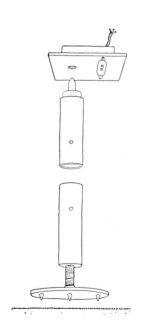

The New York showroom of the Bigelow-Sanford Carpet Company offers a kind of capsule example of many of the most significant and visible characteristics of the contemporary interior. In spite of the fact that this is a highly specialized installation, intended for the display and selection of floor coverings, the devices used for this purpose are exactly the same as those used in museums, commercial interiors and houses.

The lighting consists largely of recessed fixtures, bullets and spots. Partitions are free of the ceiling, and, in many instances, set above the floor as well. There is a system of demountable supports which closely resembles many of the structures shown in an earlier section of the book. The drawing at the left shows the basic design—an aluminum pole which seats itself in a ceiling plate. There are 175 of these plates in the showroom, each mounted on an outlet box so that power may be taken off for adjustable lighting units. A broad floor plate with prongs on the bottom guarantees that the pole, once set correctly, will stay that way, and, as is standard in such supports, there is a device for putting the pole in compression. As used in the showroom, the system is for supporting display panels and screens and for holding spotlights.

The over-all effect of space and freedom, while typical of modern interiors in general, seems entirely appropriate in this context. Carpet displays, which are bulky at best, are arranged here with adequate visibility and plenty of room around them. In the seating areas such as the one shown in the photograph there are enough display facilities to remind relaxing buyers that this is a carpet showroom and not merely a lounge. Designers: Donald Deskey Associates. Project staff: Ralph Gulley, Dana Cole, Arthur Finn, John Pile, Stanley Reese, J. Frederick Woerner, Jr., Frank Wallis.

Fran Byrne

This showroom to display resilient flooring for Congoleum-Nairn in Chicago, offers still another example of the rapidly growing use of light metal structures for interiors. Generally speaking, both purpose and practice in these installations tend to be pretty much the same: the original large open space remains open, and the structures for displays, partitions, lighting units, etc., provide what is needed with flexibility.

The system used here is somewhat more complex than most for it involves the integration of vertical members with a special ceiling grid of metal channels, also used for acoustical tile and recessed lighting fixtures. The larger of the drawings shows a section through a display unit which appears in the photograph at the extreme right, and it illustrates the manner in which the upright engages the ceiling channel. The floor piece can also be used as a top support where a ceiling channel is not in the desired position. As in many of the other systems, an adjustable screw connector sets the post into position. Designer: Reuben Sabetay of Sabetay Associates.

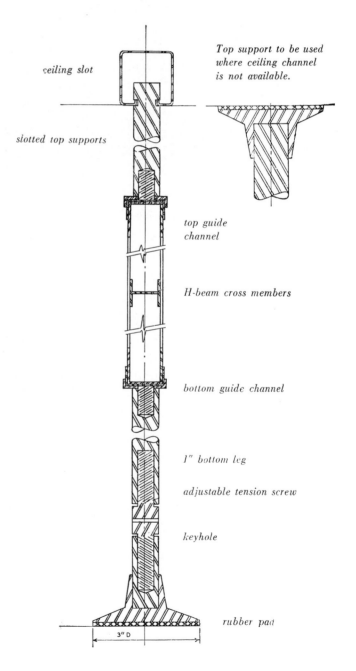

ceiling slot

Top support to be used where ceiling channel is not available.

slotted top supports

top guide channel

H-beam cross members

bottom guide channel

1" bottom leg

adjustable tension screw

keyhole

rubber pad

3" D

In the resilient flooring industry there have long
been traditional display methods—note the vertical
rolls of linoleum at rear of photograph—but devices introduced in other fields are finding their
way in. Here, in an Armstrong Cork Company
showroom, is a panel display based on the angle
of vision. Designer: Morris Lapidus.

Gottscho-Schleisner

Display methods employed for materials whose ultimate use is in the form of large flat areas depend
to a great extent on the space available to the designer. Ideally, the way to show any material or
product is in some association with its destination: it would be most convenient if one could select
a rug by trying full-size samples in the actual room, but this is rarely feasible. Showroom design,
therefore, invariably represents some kind of compromise.

The Italian design above, executed for Filiale in Milan, is an extreme example of the materials
display which makes no effort to simulate conditions of use. The showroom space was too small to
permit any of the conventional display techniques and, the designer therefore took the firm's linoleum
and rubber tile samples as elements of interior design and made the room, itself, the display. A
geometric mural by painters Dova and Ballocco forms one long wall, while simpler patterns make up
the others and the floor. This use of the product is ingenious and effective, but from the viewpoint of
merchandising a good deal would depend on the imagination of the customer. Designer: Marco Zanuso.

Showroom by Baughman-Lee, Los Angeles, for Milo Baughman furniture, Olga Lee fabrics and wallpapers.

Room setting to show furniture and tiles. House of Italian Handicrafts, New York.

Exhibition of Japanese furniture. Mitsukoshi department store, Tokyo

The extraordinary upsurge of interest in furniture since the end of the war has not only resulted in the appearance of a remarkable variety of furniture designs, but in a corresponding increase of interest in its display. As suggested by the illustrations, this interest in international in its scope. Even in Japan (left) where furniture of the Western variety has been virtually non-existent for centuries, there has been a sudden emergence of pieces for sitting, dining, etc., and displays have been widely held and heavily attended. The photograph above suggests something of the range of current Italian work—from traditional handicraft designs to sleek constructions in wood and metal.

P. A. De

Normally the background of a furniture display is a fixed affair, designed for installation in a specific location. This example, and a number which follow, represents another aspect of the general problem—the creation of an exhibit to travel or to be shown for a very short period. The room shown above is in the former category and it was photographed as installed in one of a number of department stores. Requirements of any circulating exhibition are that it be easy to erect, take down and ship. In this instance, the solution involved the use of light poles, removable shelving, flat sheets (expanded metal for the ceiling, plywood for display panels) and easily packed fabrics. The exhibit was largely devoted to Swedish knock-down furniture, and it was designed by Knoll Associates who also distributed the furniture.

Wheaton Galentine

An exhibit at the 1952 Home Furnishings Show in Grand Central Palace, for the Baker Furniture company. The pieces shown are all designs by Finn Juhl, the Danish designer who has become widely known for his highly personal developments of the Scandinavian tradition in furniture design. The booth has been designed as an all-white box in which the display pieces are, so to speak, floated. The texture of the rear wall has been produced with flat plywood cutouts in the characteristic shapes of Juhl's furniture. An interesting feature, not of the display, but of the furniture itself, is the use of double hanging strips to which the narrow cases are attached; these demonstrate in a simple and effective manner the flexibility in height possible with this arrangement. Upholstered chairs and the sofa are covered in brightly colored Siamese silks. Display design: Warner-Leeds.

A room display at the Baltimore Museum of Art, designed by Edward Wormley. The two-level scheme makes clear the separation of the area into living and dining sections and presents to the viewer a good sampling of furniture designed by Wormley for the Dunbar Furniture company. The exhibit was conceived and built as a complete set with the object of producing as realistic an illusion of an actual room as was possible.

Elmer L. Astleford

The "For Modern Living" exhibit held at the Detroit Institute of Arts in 1949 was the most complete of its kind ever held in this country. Designed by Alexander Girard, it involved a total transformation of the central core of the museum and presented in a remarkably dramatic manner the work of many of the nation's outstanding designers in the form of furniture, accessories and complete rooms. Views of a number of installations are shown on pages 144 to 147. The photograph above indicates the length to which the design was carried to establish suitable settings for the furniture on display. Here, in the museum's main court, a completely landscaped garden and terrace section were set up to permit the proper exhibition of outdoor furniture. The illustrations that follow show a number of the rooms created by different designers under Girard's direction.

Elmer L. Astleford

The space designed by Charles Eames for the Detroit Institute exhibit is not so much a literal presentation of a room as the expression of an attitude, conveyed through the use of a special personal vocabulary. The main "carrier" of this expression, aside from the furniture itself, is a wall studded with pegs on which a miscellaneous assortment of objects is hung—a large photograph, a pot of flowers, a mask, a kite. The wall and its treatment suggest not only the possibility of endlessly arranging and rearranging its contents, but the desirability of so doing. Furniture includes many of the familiar pieces produced by the Herman Miller Furniture Company, and an experimental unit, the molded plastic chaise, which has yet to be put into production. Lighting is produced by two sources—the decorative cluster at the right, and a grid of reflector lamps set into standard conduit which is treated as part of the over-all display. The floor is spattered to suggest the effect of a terrazzo, and the main color at this level comes from the rug and the two fabric-covered boxes. While not at all a room in the conventional sense, the space definitely does suggest an approach to the problem of the small interior.

continued

This living-dining area designed by Florence Knoll suggests solutions to the problem of a space set aside for general family use. One continuous wall contains a variety of storage places, including a drop-leaf desk and a small bar. An off-center fireplace (left) has a raised hearth which can be used for extra seating, or as a place for setting glasses and ash trays. The freestanding desk in the foreground of the illustration above is by Franco Albini, the Italian architect-designer.

Materials throughout the space have been chosen to withstand reasonably heavy use: typical is the use of a butcher's block for the coffee table, laminated plastic for the dining top, leather, washable sailcloth and plastic covers. Here, as in the Eames room on the preceding page, the designer worked toward an effective display which also suggested possibilities for interior treatment. The intent was not to produce a room which was necessarily to be repeated in facsimile.

photos: Elmer L. Astleford

Unlike the preceding examples, this room, another of the displays in the Detroit museum show, could be translated into an actual living space with a minimum of modification. Even here, however, it can be seen that display requirements strongly conditioned the design. The space made available to the designer, George Nelson, was well below the eye level of the spectators (see railing at extreme left, above) and maximum emphasis was therefore given the facing wall. This area was filled with a storage wall, using components manufactured by the Herman Miller Furniture Company, and provision was made for books, radio and record player, writing materials and miscellaneous objects. The room is of interest for its almost complete lack of portable furniture: a light armchair at the desk, a small stand at the built-in couch, and that is all. At the end (right) there is a variation on the theme of the Hawaiian *hikia*, here treated as a hard platform with space for a mattress and pillows, and plants.

*Eero Saarinen, designer with
Florence Knoll and Herbert Matter.
Chair from Knoll Associates.*

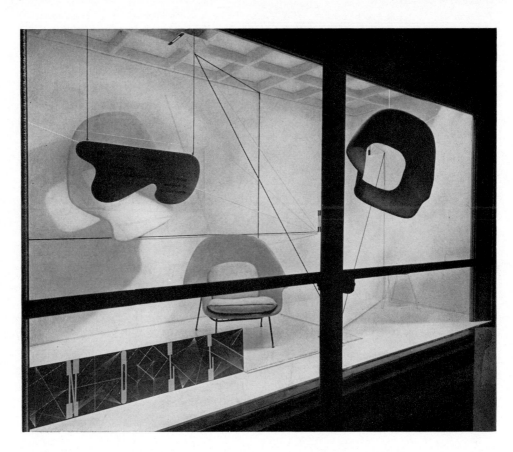

The show windows on these two pages are the result of an interesting experiment by the Chicago department store of Carson, Pirie, Scott and Company. In connection with the display of a number of lines of modern furniture, the store commissioned the designers to do the windows as well. Each, naturally, was given a window for the display of his own furniture designs. No limitations were set except those of reasonable practicality and window size.

Two of the designers Saarinen and Eames chose to treat their windows as semi-abstract three-dimensional compositions, and each relied on the furniture forms themselves for the shapes used as decoration. In each instance this approach worked effectively because the designers were concerned with the display of individual items.

The other two windows illustrated, by Nelson and Wormley were used to show a variety of related pieces of furniture and hence had to be set up as groups. The Wormley window presents a convincingly complete room setting; the design by Nelson implies a room setting vy the grouping of the various pieces, but in actuality the background contains nothing more than areas of flat color.

The variety of solutions to this show window problem, as seen in the work of these four designers, indicates that even objects as large and unwieldy as furniture can be incorporated into relatively small displays with uncommon impact.

George Nelson and Associates, designer.
Furniture from Herman Miller.

Edward J. Wormley, designer.
Furniture from Dunbar.

Charles Eames, designer.
Furniture from Herman Miller.

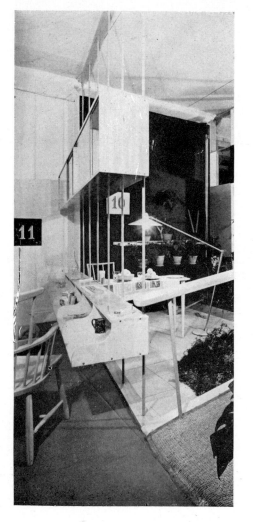

The various aspects of a department store exhibit illustrated on these two pages add up to an intelligent and showmanlike evaluation of the problem by the designers, Roger and Robert Nicholson. The problem had two aspects: it was the desire of Britain's Council of Industrial Design to present what had been done in portable lamps and lighting units in such a way as to stimulate manufacturers to produce better merchandise; and, at the same time, to so upgrade public tastes that such merchandise would be demanded. The devices by which these requirements were met are interesting. Since the lamp or lighting fixture does not normally exist in isolation, it was not shown here detached from the kind of setting in which it might be found—the exhibit contains both furnishings and the suggestions of backgrounds. But since the problem was to illustrate lighting possibilities and not room settings, the latter were handled in such a way that there would be no confusion in the mind of the beholder: the settings are frankly exhibit backgrounds and not reproductions of interiors. To emphasize the domestic character of the display, the store's high ceilings were masked out by lower ceilings of stretched muslin. And to insure that the main point of the exhibit be clearly understood, all lighting is by the units on display.

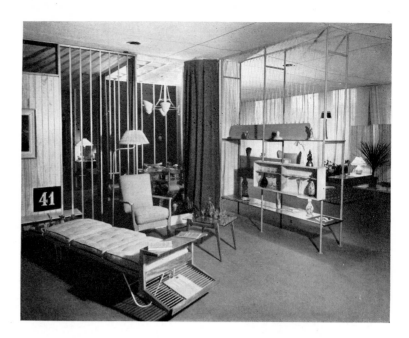

Where a wall is required by the furniture arrangement it is generally suggested by a framework of light studs.

Everything in the exhibit is relevant. As an example, the panel of leaf forms at the left is used as an enlargement of the pattern on the shade of hanging lamp 5.

A plank attached to poles makes a "ceiling" for a hanging lamp. To suggest a window, the designers used a net of metal covered with vines.

photos: Studio Swain

The open shelf structures are occasionally filled in with panels to simulate cabinets or cupboards. Each piece of furniture (many types are represented) is related to an appropriate lamp.

Wilming

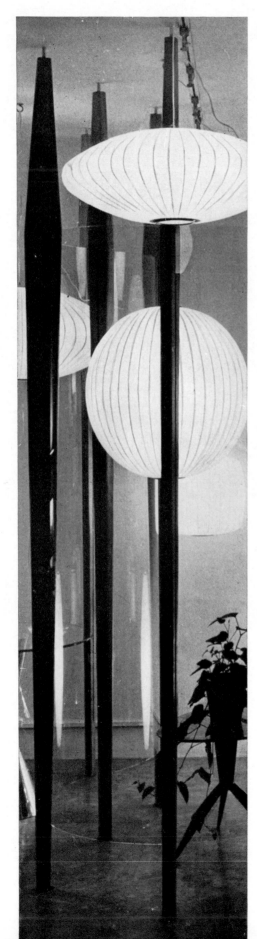

Two methods of displaying hanging lamps, used in the Chicago and New York showrows of Raymor (Richard Morgenthau). The upper photograph shows a relatively conventional arrangement; below, a display of George Nelson's plastic-skinned Bubble lamps which fills a space from floor to ceiling.

G. Barrows

The problem of a wholesale showroom for household accessories and gift items is one which has baffled more than one designer. The difficulty lies in the multiplicity of objects which vary greatly in use and size. The designer's job is to house a great quantity of merchandise, give each group effective display, and still keep the showroom relatively clean and uncluttered. One of the best solutions to date is Edward J. Wormley's showrooms for Raymor, and one of many ingenious devices he employed is shown above. Ceramics, clocks, lamps and other objects are set out on glass shelves bracketed to metal poles; the device which provides individual display for groups is a series of cloth fins. Easily cleaned or changed, these colorful dividers perform their function effectively and inexpensively.

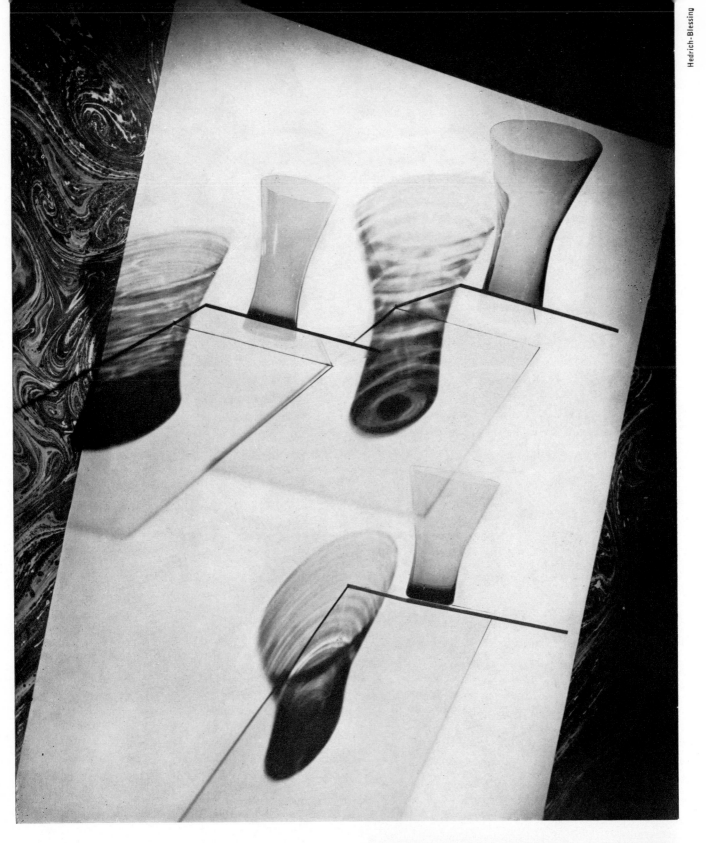

Two views of the section devoted to glass and ceramics at the 1952 "Good Design" show in the Merchandise Mart. The main background, a bold marble pattern by Laverne, was also one of the selections for the show. The display table in the foreground is a large sheet of glass supported by four tripods, themselves part of the furniture selected for display by the jury. The standards of display set in these Good Design shows has been very high indeed, and other installations are shown more comprehensively elsewhere in the book. Designer of the 1952 exhibit was Paul Rudolph.

A small and extremely restrained exhibit designed by Philip Johnson for the Museum of Modern Art in New York. Subject of the display was a collection of the elegant, delicate glass produced by Lobmeyr. Backgrounds are of gray, gold and white marbleized paper, and many of the shelves are covered in black or gray shantung. The total simplicity of the display and the choice of materials do much to enhance the fragile beauty of the glass itself.

An open storage wall with glass shelves, used for the display of ceramics and glassware in the Chicago shop of Baldwin Kingrey. Designer: Harry Weese.

It is generally accepted that in the field of exhibition and display, the designers of Switzerland and Italy have consistently led the world. It was not surprising, therefore, to find that the exhibit at Italy's 1951 Milan Triennale which aroused the most discussion was Swiss. This interior, which displayed a variety of products from Switzerland, was a jet-black room with nothing in it but waist-high showcases. Shaped like drums, and internally lighted, the stands formed oval pools of light in the darkness and most effectively called attention to the products they contained. The designer Max Bill is also known for his work in architecture, sculpture, industrial and graphic design.

Oval trays hung on a metal column are used as display surfaces
in the Gallery of Glass at the 1951 Triennale at Milan. The
oval shape is a pleasant one when combined with the glassware
forms, and an interesting variety is developed by changing the
point of attachment to the column. Architect: Roberto Menghi.
Designers: Elio Palazzo and Gian Luigi Reggio. For other
photographs see page 176.

The display at the right was designed by Gyorgy Kepes for a
Christmas show of ceramics and accessories at Boston's Institute
of Contemporary Art. The scheme adopted is simple but extremely effective: the crisp shades of the objects are in dramatic
contrast to the rough bed of rocks and pebbles.

The display of home accessories and giftwares has come a long way in the few years since the war. Traditionally this kind of merchandise has been arranged on the simple basis of cramming as much of everything as could be squeezed on available shelves and tables. The most recent of the retail shops in this field, however, have adopted the procedures used in exhibitions to call attention to the wares.

A typical and well-executed example is the 20th Century Shop in New Orleans, designed by James Lamantia. In this shop the constructivist techniques formerly associated only with sculpture and stage design have been employed to form surfaces and containers for display. The use of standard metal hanging strips suggests an economical kind of flexibility.

An interior in the House of Italian Handicrafts, a showroom in New York, which is of particular current interest because of the important work of contemporary designers in the fields of furniture, glass, ceramics and lighting. As backgrounds for the displays, designs by a number of Italian architects were used; in this illustration, the work of Ernesto Rogers and Ignazio Gardella. The main display structures are perforated uprights which take standard shelf brackets, a system not unlike several manufactured in this country. The general scheme is typical of much current design in Italy: a simplicity verging on bareness, with decorative accents provided by strongly emphasized mechanical features—in this case, the display structures and the adjustable floor lamps.

Ben Schnall

More than many new shops, this inexpensive conversion of one floor in a New York brownstone house exemplifies what has happened to display design in many types of retail establishments. The "show window," for instance, has ceased to exist. It has been replaced inside by a shop whose entire interior has been conceived as a show window, and outside by a showcase on stilts. The blurring of the formerly sharp line between inside and out, which appears to work so well for many kinds of retail stores, is justified on many counts by its proponents. It gives the shop as a whole greater visibility, it provides for a larger variety of possible displays and it is effective in attracting customers since visible barriers to entry do not exist. However, it might also be recalled that this development is characteristic of more than retail store design: exactly the same evolution—for different reasons—has taken place in houses and a variety of other building types. Transparency, in other words, has become a desirable attribute of contemporary design regardless of the function to be met. Designer: Norman Cherner Associates.

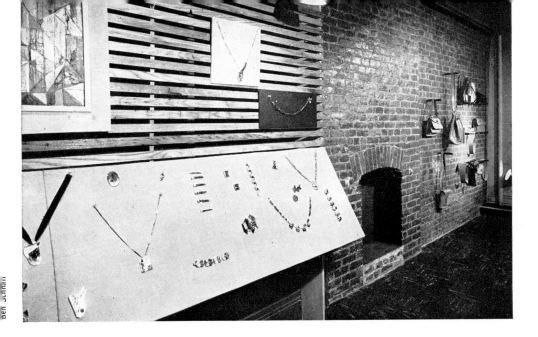

Another view of the Idella La Vista shop which handles costume jewelry, handbags and accessories, treating all of its merchandise as a problem in display. The jewelry, for example, is displayed in the open on a long easel panel covered with yellow felt. The chestnut slats above provide a change in texture and additional display opportunities.

A jewelry display in the Carol Antell shop designed by Seymour Joseph. By reducing the usual glass counter displays to circular wells, greatly increased emphasis is given the merchandise. Such treatment applies most appropriately where the merchandise has a relatively high unit value.

One of the designer's chief advantages in the display of small objects—freedom to organize the material in almost any desired manner—is also one of the major problems. If the subject matter of an exhibit were, say, tractors and heavy excavation equipment, the designer would be greatly limited by the bulk and weight of the individual items, but the character of the display would almost automatically be established by the objects themselves. Here, as in all exhibits dealing with a multiplicity of small things, the subject matter approaches invisibility even at short distances, and unless something is done in the space itself to suggest the nature of the display, the possibility of dramatic emphasis is lost. The space illustrated above is the gold, silverware and jewelry section at the Milan Triennale of 1951, and it offers several interesting examples of ways in which to approach the problem. The space itself has been made into an interior of great elegance with curtains extending from floor to ceiling and a room-height painting by Taiuti. Directly above the cases (themselves designs suggesting the value of their contents) is set a horizontal panel which, like a low ceiling, reduces the scale and accents the display. The wall panel behind consists of Italian portraits of the Renaissance showing heavily jeweled ladies as another way of stating the theme of the display. Finally, it should be observed how all of these elements combine to focus attention on the cases. The solution is brilliantly developed, and one should not be misled by its seeming simplicity. Designers were a painter-architect team, Umberto Zimelli and Renato G. Angeli.

The exhibit shown below is another type of solution to the problem discussed on the facing page. Again, small objects to be displayed in a large room; again, the conditions of large-scale public display as contrasted with the more controllable environment of a small shop. In this exhibit, "Jewelry under Fifty Dollars" at the Walker Art Center in Minneapolis, the scheme developed is a regular spacing of square panels, hung against a background of vertical strips, also regularly spaced. Each panel is covered with bright-colored wool, and each is protected by a slanting glass front set into side fins. Photographic panels, such as the screen at the left, supplement the display. It would be difficult to make a fair comparison between the two very different answers presented on these pages. One is an international exhibit, obviously developed with a generous budget; the other is a limited show for local audiences, displaying a fair quality of inexpensive merchandise. What does emerge very clearly from the comparison is the extreme range of possible solutions. Designer: Hilde Reiss.

A perfume shop in Milan which demonstrates the capacity of the best Italian designers when it comes to developing a concept to its limit. Here the merchandise is a luxury article, and the entire shop makes this explicit. Highly polished surfaces and costly materials are visible everywhere—in the large-scale terrazzo of the floor, in the glass tile wall, in the gleaming counter. Lighting is treated as decorative structure rather than as functional equipment, and the variation in design of the three groups of fixtures suggests that everything in the shop is in a one-of-a-kind category. A full-height mirror wall at the rear adds another high-gloss surface and duplicates the dazzling interior. Display units are treated casually, almost as an afterthought, and the great bulk of the merchandise is kept out of sight. Designer: Ernesto Carboni.

Above and at left, details of the perfume shop. Note the slight changes in direction of the counter, the lighting below it, the carefully scattered recessed display cases. The shop front is open only at the door, and great emphasis is placed on the name which is back-lighted and set out from a strongly textured background.

Many of the examples in this section are by contemporary Italian architects and designers, and one of the reasons is that there is much to be learned from them. Current work on shops, exhibits and displays is at as high a level in Italy as anywhere in the world; and within the general framework of their style, the designers show extraordinary versatility and individuality. One explanation of the extreme range of Italian work lies in the nature of the industry which serves the designers and their clients. There exists very little in the way of standard, mass-produced equipment and fittings, and hence there are few opportunities for the architect or designer to "design out of a catalogue," as is so commonly done here. Along with this situation there is its corollary: the presence of a large number of small, semi-handicraft workshops which produce lighting fixtures and equipment, hardware, show-cases and so on. Due to a traditionally low wage scale and the lack of price comparisons with industrially produced items, there is every incentive for the Italian designer to use special designs throughout. This explains to some extent the remarkable variety of Italian display design but not the quality of imagination so often revealed. The leather shop for Valigeria Franzi in Milan, by Carlo De Carli illustrates one characteristic of many of the best designers: a preoccupation with structure used as decoration, expressed with great freedom and boldness. The problem in the leather shop was the creation of display cases at the window, and the architect used this requirement as an opportunity to create a striking construction which entirely dominates the shop interior, whether seen from inside or out. Other examples of this kind of approach will be found elsewhere in the book.

The influence of the automobile on the design of store fronts is not one to be lightly discounted or overlooked. To some extent the open front is a reflection of a desire to attract the attention of the motorized passer-by, and in some instances, as here, the effect is very clear. This is one of the stores of the May Company in the Los Angeles area, and it is located on an important traffic artery. The building is four stories in height, completely open for its full length at street level and virtually windowless above. Displays are set on a platform which also runs for the length of the open front, and they are backed up by a counter-height unit which serves the double function of storage and of opening the view to the rest of the interior. The designer confronted with window display space of this size has a problem very different from that of the small shop: the ingenious space-saving displays appropriate for the latter must give way to techniques of mass exhibit. The function is more to reveal the nature and quantity of the merchandise than the specific details which would be lost on the crowds going by in automobiles. Designers: Albert C. Martin & Associates. Associated architects: Marx, Flint and Schonne.

In this men's shop in Long Beach, California, the architects
designed the front so that it would stand out sharply in an in-
tensely competitive area, and the devices used to achieve this are
of interest. Most important is the impression of unusual depth,
created by carrying out the eggcrate ceiling to the edge of the shop
overhang. This alone makes it hard to establish the position of
the glass front and gives the shop windows an apparent depth
which includes the overhang. Setting the glass into the brick piers
without visible metal moldings heightens the illusion. By letting
the piers run up through the ceiling and by keeping the other
backgrounds low, the impression of depth is further emphasized.
The angled windows are a familiar device for increasing visibility
of displays. Designers: Gruen and Krummeck.

There are two ways to evaluate the display set-up in this window of Libreria dello Stato in Milan: functionally it appears entirely adequate, but in meeting the requirements, the designer has gone far beyond a purely functional solution. From the point of view of the passer-by, the way in which books and prints have been displayed is admirable, for each shelf is tilted for easy reading of titles, and the entire height of the show window has been utilized. It is also possible to see into the shop over the low barrier of slatted doors. As a design, however, the scaffolding reflects the current Italian tendency to romanticize structures, carrying the shaping of members to the point where the effect is that of sculpture. Ico Parisi, the designer of the shop, has also done furniture in much the same vein, using exquisite craftsmanship in the complicated modeling of the various members. Despite its somewhat extravagant appearance, this shelf scaffold is closely related to a broad design trend in so much modern work, most simply described as "a cage within a shell." This has been evident in the section on light metal structures for shops and showrooms and in much of the exhibition work shown here. In this respect the Parisi shop design is especially interesting for it indicates one of the extremes to which the general concept can be carried when developed by a talented and highly individual dsigner.

The Cantoni bookshop in Milan suffered bomb damage during the war, and in its present state shows an economical redesign by the internationally known firm of Banfi, Belgiojoso, Peressutti and Rogers. Again we see an expression of the "cage within a shell," here developed as a ladderlike scaffolding which facilitates the rearrangement of displays, and, yet keeps open a view of the shop.

The Golden Griffin, in New York, is notable for the way in which it stands out from its neighbors although its size verges on the microscopic. Located on a corner, the store has its main window set back from the building line so that the front column stands free. Although the setback represented a real loss of space, for so small a shop, it definitely enhances the display and offers an invitation to stop and look. The window display is the complete interior. Books set in the window are arranged on light, low stands to preserve the open effect. Lighting is both direct and indirect and is maintained at a high level to give a maximum of visibility from both streets. Architects: Antonin Raymond and L. L. Rado. Consultant designer: Ladislav Sutnar.

It is traditional, in the selling of books, for the shop to do everything possible to encourage customers to come in and browse. For this reason the bookstore plan rarely includes counters behind which the customer cannot go, or any other barriers to free circulation. The three shops on these pages show quite vividly in what way the tradition has been preserved and developed through use of the contemporary technique of display. The glass wall, giving a full view of the interior, is one important element, and the playing down of window displays as such, is another.

The Bonniers shop in New York, as originally designed by Warner-Leeds, was one of the most distinguished of these solutions, and it is of special interest because merchandise included more than books. As set up until very recently, the book department took up most of the street-level sales and display space, while glass, china, silver, etc., were located on the second. It was this mixed requirement which led to the design of a show window which opens up the shop at both floor levels. After the shop had been in operation for some time, a management decision led to the elimination of books in favor of gifts, household accessories and furniture. It was then adapted by its owner to meet the new requirements, but on this and the following pages, the shop is shown as originally designed.   *continued*

This is the interior view of the window display at Bonniers seen from the front of the second floor which is set back from the glass and stopped by a thin railing. It is this setback which articulates the two-story scheme both inside and out, simultaneously expressing structure, space relationships and scheme. The clearance created by the setback allows use of the full two-story height for display. In this area the ceiling is of wood and has attached to it the hardware for the hanging of lamps, fabrics, panels, etc., as required. The heavy wood uprights in the show window itself are provided with pins which receive angled shelves (as shown below) and horizontal ones in glass (see previous page) on which books, pottery, silver and other items can be arranged. Much of the distinction of the Bonniers shop stems from the apparent ease with which an entire complex of activities has been integrated and expressed: the two-story scheme is perfectly evident inside and out, the relationship of display and selling areas has been beautifully worked out, and the way in which the two-story interior has been combined with a generally open plan is admirable. It seems possible that in shops of this sort, where the line between window display and interior architecture is so thin, there may be new problems as well as new possibilities for the window dresser. Without a sealed background against which to work, the display designer has to have a real sympathy for the contemporary interior as well as a working knowledge of his trade.

Wheaton Galentine

In a shop whose interiors and displays are so closely inter-related, it is easier to show fragments of spaces in photographs than to capture the essential atmosphere of the place. The view above shows a corner of the stair well and the second floor looking towards the front. Right, another second floor view in the same direction, but showing the visual relationship between the two floors. Note the use of display cases glazed on both sides to give visibility to their contents from both levels and the stair.

continued

One of the special details at Bonniers is the adjustable display unit for large art books
and magazines. A slatted affair constructed of strips of birch fastened to a panel, it
is set out from the wall at an angle. Variation in the displays is accomplished by
inserting wood strips between the slats as required by the number and size of the
publications to be shown. No screws or other fastening devices are required. The
hanging lamp which furnishes direct light for the panel is part of the merchandise
sold in the shop, and its use here thus has double value. Designers of the shop, Warner-
Leeds, also designed all the display-storage units.

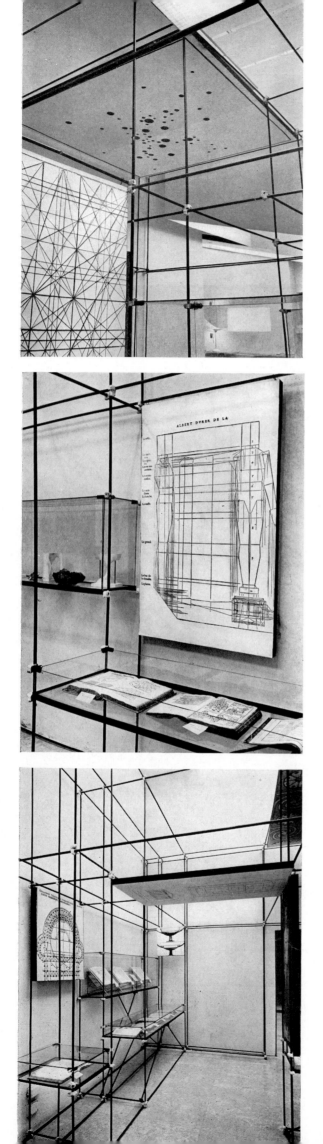

In one section of the Milan Triennale of 1951 there was a small exhibit devoted to the subject of Harmony and Proportion. Theories on this subject have intermittently fascinated artists and designers for centuries, and any number of attempts have been made to establish mathematical and other basis for proper proportions. Dürer devoted a great deal of time to the problem, as did Leonardo da Vinci. In more recent times Jay Hambidge spent years on his theory of "Dynamic Symmetry," based on study of Attic vases and Doric temples, and Le Corbusier has worked out his own system, the "Modulor." All this adds up to a subject remarkable for its complexity, abstruseness and lack of interest to the great majority of people and yet, despite the difficulties presented by the subject matter, the designer of this exhibit has developed a display which is both entertaining and appropriate. The system is again a cage, assembled with metal rods and connectors reminiscent of those used with laboratory equipment. There is great variety in the placing of the cases, charts and display panels (proportions are faithful to the "Golden Section") and an easy kind of delicacy. It is exhibition design of this quality which has put the modern Italian designers at the top of the field. Architect: Francesco Gnecchi-Ruscone.

The undulating ceiling of wood slats is a device first used for acoustical reasons by Alvar Aalto in his famous library at Viipuri. Here it serves to take care of inconvenient projections in the old ceiling, and to help minimize the effect of an excessively deep and narrow space. Lighting is a combination of fluorescent, in the form of exposed tubing, and ceiling mounted floods and spots. There is no evidence of any effort to either conceal the lighting or to make it "decorative." In this deliberate articulation of functional elements the space also resembles much Italian work. On the long west wall (below) the architects combined display panels and cases with the desks and chairs necessary for interviews. By combining these many diverse elements an impression of unity is gained and the number of distractions is reduced. George Kadleigh was associated with James Cubitt and Partners in the design of the South African Tourist Corporation.

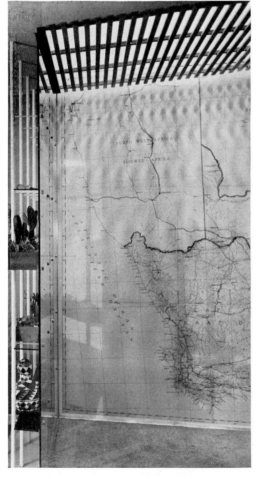

photos: Alfred Cracknell

These two offices in London were designed by the same firm of architects, James Cubitt and Partners. The bureau for the South African Tourist Corporation was commissioned first, the other somewhat later. The problem of how best to compete with one's own job, while slighting neither client, is an interesting one; and perhaps it is just as well that architects are not impaled on this particular dilemma too often.

The South Africa office, when published in the *Architectural Review*, was described as "the most advanced and imaginative example of the disappearing shop front to be carried out in London to date." Considering the reserve with which this publication handles its material, this is high praise but by no means excessive. The architects have taken a familiar situation—the long, narrow shop space of a dilapidated building—and have produced a most distinguished solution. The distinction, incidentally, does not lie in the originality of the design, but in its assured maturity. Every element is one used many times before: the idea of the unframed, all-glass front, the marble side wall which crosses the invisible barrier between inside and out, the undulating ceiling, the floor with many different patterns and textures, the maner in which displays have been handled and so on. Not shown here, unfortunately, is the fresh and wholly effective use of color: the yellow and green in the sign backgrounds, the contrast of warm sycamore in the ceiling and dark green marble in the side wall at the entrance, the bright spots in pink and blue scattered through the floor. This design succeeds most admirably in combining a relaxed solution and functional requirements with an atmosphere of quiet gaiety. One suspects that many Londoners must make inquiries about South Africa only to enjoy this interior. The adjoining facade for Qantas Empire Airways is, by deliberate contrast, more conservative in its use of glass and the interior is, in addition, screened from direct view. For the treatment of the side around the corner, see the following pages.

photos: Alfred Cracknell

The two photographs on this page are interior and exterior views of the same window wall. The open slat ceiling which screens the fluorescent tubes is made of sycamore slats, selected to relate to the ceiling of the same material in the South Africa office next door. The photographs also show the relationship between the furniture and the metal-frame display cases.

The Qantas space differs from that of its neighbor in that it is small and square (rather than deep and narrow), located on a corner and plagued with a number of existing columns in inconvenient places. Because the space was small, the architects decided to screen both fronts as a way of suggesting greater depth. Because of the corner site, the main front was placed on the street away from the South Africa office, thus reducing competition between the two and opening up the Qantas office to views from other directions. The main front (facing page) consists of an intermittent screen formed by suspended cases filled with appropriate displays. These are brightly lighted from the top by a row of reflector lamps at the ceiling with cylindrical baffles to concentrate the illumination. The major lighting, furnished by cold cathode tubes, is partly screened by a hung ceiling. A mirror (see facing photograph) serves to increase the feeling of space by its reflection of the ceiling slats. There is a certain consistency throughout the design which creates a sense of importance out of proportion to the actual size of the office. The fact that the owners felt strongly enough about it to have everything including furniture, displays and accessories designed—or carefully selected—communicates itself instantly to the observer. The difference between distinguished and mediocre interiors is often less a matter of "design" alone than an insistence on the complete development of the job, down to its least important details. James Cubitt and Partners, architects.

One characteristic of Italian design which has called forth more comment than almost any other is its singular grace and elegance, and it is when this quality emerges in connection with the display and sale of office machines that it takes on special interest for U. S. designers who are accustomed to think of this particular problem in quite different terms.

The Frassi showroom in Milan, which handles both typewriters and calculating machines, occupies the ground floor of an old masonry building. The attempt to achieve an open front consequently carried through only as far as the existing structure permitted; even so the shop successfully functions as its own display window, and the extreme delicacy of the metal sash is in striking and agreeable contrast with the rusticated stone facade. Inside, the designer has treated the merchandise in a way one might have expected if it were jewelry or expensive perfumes. Each typewriter, each adding machine has its own predetermined location; and, in some instances, its own private lighting fixture. A planting strip under one of the display shelves contributes to the effect of expensive elegance, as does the floor of very unbusinesslike Venetian mosaic.

That this approach should be adopted for the display of this type of merchandise is revealing and stimulating when viewed in terms of U. S. practices. Office machines are not jewelry, but at their best they are remarkably handsome, and often costly. A setting like this makes such qualities readily apparent. Architect: Marco Zanuso.

The use of exposed lighting fixtures as an important visual element in the interior is typical of much current work in Italy, adds interest and richness. The mosaic floor is traditional: as used here it is of major importance in distinguishing this showroom from the general run of commercial display spaces. The three-tiered table is a device which functions better and looks better than a single broad table top.

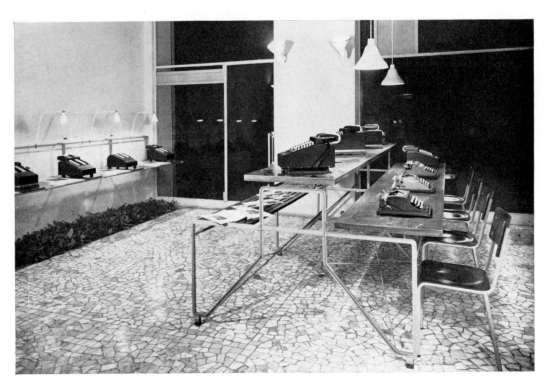

The Olivetti Company, manufacturer of typewriters, calculators and other office machines, has undoubtedly had more to do with Italy's high reputation in the field of industrial design than almost all others put together. The company's design program, discussed briefly on the facing page, carries through all its activities, including even housing and community planning, and has set quality standards unsurpassed anywhere. Three of the Olivetti shops, located in Forli, Brussels and Savonia (below) are illustrated here. While they vary in size and plan to conform with local situations, the basic schemes are standard: lettering on signs is uniform, and nothing ever appears except the company name; shop contents are always handled as if they were in an exhibit space; backgrounds are uniformly simple; each shop has a maximum opening on the front which permits the whole interior to register as a show window. Designer: Gian Antonio Bernasconi.

The remarkable accomplishments of Olivetti—and its chief designer Marcello Nizzoli—were given recognition in the U. S. in an exhibition in the Museum of Modern Art in 1952. Two things in particular distinguish the Olivetti design program: the extraordinary level of performance in all its aspects, and its complete integration. The business machines, shown on a vertical panel in the photograph above, have been universally acclaimed as the most beautiful of their kind and these alone have been sufficient to establish Nizzoli as one of the top industrial designers. Less widely known outside Italy are the related design activities of the company which include virtually everything over which it has control. The main factory at Ivrea (near Torino) is a distinguished industrial structure. Employee housing, shops, posters and advertisements are a few of the other things handled with great distinction by a sizeable group of designers and architects. Typical of the freedom and imagination with which all problems are approached is the roadside sign—a far cry from the conventional billboard—shown on the following page.

The Museum of Modern Art exhibit was designed by Leo Lionni, and its clarity, decisiveness and delicacy are completely in the spirit of the company's other activities. An interesting thing about the exhibit is that while there is material entirely suitable for three-dimensional display (the business machines, for instance) everything is attached to the walls. Whatever Lionni's reason for doing this, the result is to lead the visitor to give equal importance to everything shown, whether a typewriter, trademark or factory, and thus to make clear the company's attitude toward its entire design activity.

Three dimensional roadside sign by Giovanni Pintori

Exhibitions

*A photograph of Bayer at
the Bauhaus Exhibition he designed
for the Museum of Modern Art in 1938.
Behind the peep hole are ballet
costumes on revolving dummies*

This section of a dozen pages has been devoted to the work of Herbert Bayer for a number of excellent reasons. Bayer, perhaps more than any other designer, has developed, synthesized and expounded new ways of visual communication, and in his work in the field of exhibition and display, he has brought together a remarkable variety of techniques and media. Bayer's work is also a reminder of one of the central facts about the arts in our time: a constant expansion of activity in a steadily growing number of areas. This development has become a familiar one in the case of the industrial designer, whose claim that he can tackle the design of anything has been well documented in the past twenty-five years. What we tend to forget is that the "industrial designer" has not been a particularly trained kind of professional, but an individual who may have begun in any of a number of fields.

Herbert Bayer began as a painter and still considers himself primarily a painter. He cannot be described as an industrial designer in the same sense as the organizations which dominate that field, partly because his output has been limited by his insistence on personal control of all projects and partly because his interest has been concentrated on problems in which graphic design plays a major role. Even so, the range of his work (painting, typography, displays, graphic design, exhibitions, packaging) clearly makes the point that today's artist tends less and less to restrict himself to his easel.

Early training contributed importantly to Bayer's orientation as an artist and designer. He studied at the Bauhaus in Germany, that extraordinary institution whose influence is still felt in both design and art education, and he remained there as a teacher, in association with Gropius, Breuer and Moholy-Nagy. The Bauhaus, it will be recalled, was the first modern school to base its curriculum on the concept of the unity of all the arts, whether "fine" or otherwise, and perhaps its greatest achievement was to see this concept accepted throughout the world. It gave vital help to an entire generation of artists by teaching that while the interest in murals, monumental sculpture and easel paintings might have declined, the need for their talents in other expressions was greater than ever. Many artists, not necessarily Bauhaus products, have since demonstrated the validity of the idea—Isamu Noguchi in furniture, landscape design and lighting; Dali in display, exhibition design, jewelry and fabrics; Ben Shahn in advertising; Max Bill in a variety of fields. Among these and other examples, the exhibitions of Bayer represent a most significant contribution.

These illustrations of early work by Bayer (1928) show something of his interest in type and arrangement of flat planes, and they serve as a kind of "preview" of his later approach to the problems of exhibition design.

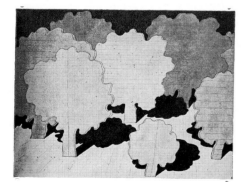

continued

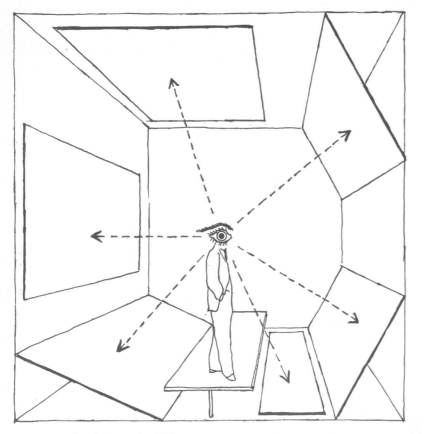

from P. M. magazine, 1939

An early exhibition idea developed by Bayer was based on the idea of the field of vision. Once expressed, the concept appeared as a very simple and obvious one: if display material is related to the height and angle of a person's vision, more can be seen simultaneously and with greater ease. A contemporary expression of similar thinking in films is the use of wide-screen techniques such as Cinerama and Cinemascope. This idea, in displays, had important consequences: it destroyed the old art gallery practice of placing pictures at eye level on flat walls and gave to the exhibition a new three-dimensional device which changed its entire character and offered new opportunities for gaining attention. In using this device—there are many examples in these pages —Bayer always respects its conditions and limitations. A good example is the show of architectural illustrations on the facing page: it is possible to hang pictures both above and below eye level as long as the proper angle of view is taken into account.

continued

The panel is of necessity the main element in all but the most special and expensive exhibitions. Bayer gives these rectangular elements a three-dimensional quality by mounting them to facilitate viewing and to focus attention. An excellent example of a simple expression of the idea is shown at the right. (Bauhaus Exhibition.)

Werkbund Exhibition, Paris (1930). Gropius, Moholy-Nagy, Breuer, Bayer.

Introductory panels at the "Road to Victory" exhibition (Museum of Modern Art, 1942). This remarkable wartime show was developed by Edward Steichen, text by Carl Sandburg and design by Herbert Bayer.

In Bayer's exhibitions, panels take many forms, fall into numerous combinations and serve a variety of functions. Above, for example, they serve to spell out the elements of a theme. At the left they not only carry subject matter, but act as a partitioning device which visually separates spectator traffic on two different levels. Below they are simple backgrounds, used only to differentiate the exhibits which are hung on them.

Bayer's exhibition devices are generally ingenious but rarely are they at all involved technically. One gets the impression that the problem is studied with extreme care and in great detail, and that the solution is allowed to develop as directly as possible. This procedure leads to results of apparent simplicity but unexpected impact. A good case in point is the exhibition detail at the right: the problem was to display a number of chairs by Mies van der Rohe and Marcel Breuer, and it was solved by taking four examples of each design and hanging them vertically. The freshness and originality of the solution is realized when one learns that the exhibition was held about twenty-five years ago. (Werkbund Exhibition)

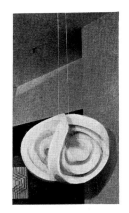

Soichi Sunami

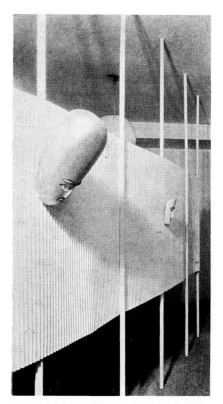

The technical simplicity mentioned on the facing page is well illustrated by the examples here. In the examples above and to the left (both from the Bauhaus show at the Museum of Modern Art) the designer's vocabulary consists of string, wood poles and corrugated paper "woven" through the supports. There is no evidence anywhere of a desire to impress, or to do anything, in fact, except present the exhibition material as effectively as possible. In the illustration below (an outdoor section of the Road to Victory exhibition) a familiar staggered screen arrangement is used to give a light structure stability, and to provide visibility from several directions.

continued

"Airways to Peace" (1943) was another Bayer show for the Museum of Modern Art; and, like its predecessor, "Road to Victory" it was conceived and executed on a monumental scale. The designer's own explanation of what he tried to do is interesting: "It was my idea to let the magic of maps and the geometry of globes give the design character. I wanted the exhibition to appear as light and bodiless as possible. Therefore, I broke down as many wall divisions as was possible without losing too much of the display area. The color of the maps was carried through in the rest of the show. The circulation again was of basic importance for the layout. The first part of the show was devoted to the history of map making, from the earliest known map of the Greek concept of their flat world, to the projections of Mercator, to the new Polar maps of the Air Age. Then followed, in pictures, the evolution of flying. . . . There was a ramp to look down upon aerial photographs. An atmosphere of geography and imaginary spaces was created by networks of ropes, screens of poles and patterns of geographical altitude lines."

Another Bayer invention for the show was this transparent globe. By sighting past a point at the center the opposite point on the globe could immediately be located.

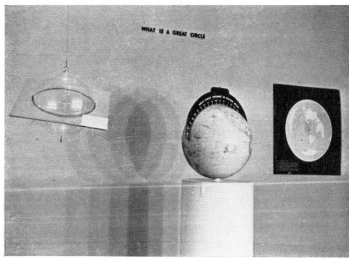

An essential of the Bayer technique is to focus attention by showing familiar material in unexpected ways. Main feature of this exhibition was a globe turned inside out (opposite page) and suspended from the ceiling. Its concave inner surface showed the relationship between land masses and oceans at a glance. This admirably direct device has a particularly appropriate use in this instance, but the reader will recognize its derivation in the early "field of vision" diagram on page 110. The ramp below also has a justifiable function—it also happens to be one of Bayer's favorite exhibition devices.

continued

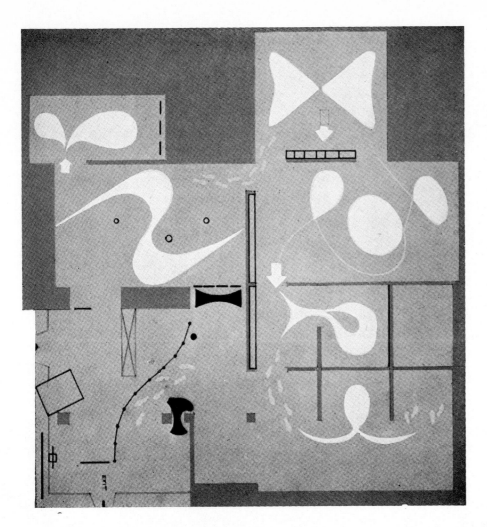

entrance

At the Bauhaus exhibition, Bayer guided the spectators not only by the use of screens and partitions but also by painted flow patterns on the floor. The only difficulty with this device is that white paint on gray concrete is almost impossible to maintain, and the crowds of the first few days greatly reduced its effectiveness.

Museum of Modern Art

"Flow is derived from theme; layout from flow." There has been a good bit of controversy among designers about the relative desirability of controlled flow versus free movement of spectators, and it should be apparent by now that Bayer feels very strongly that it is up to the designer to decide in which way exhibition material is to be viewed. For him, an exhibition has a story to tell. The story begins at the entrance and ends at the exit, and it should be seen—just as a book is read—in its proper sequence. Thus, exhibition design first requires that the material be organized in its proper order, and then placed so that traffic flow corresponds with the unfolding of the story. The floor plan, in other words, is nothing more than an accurate reflection of the story sequence. This is why, in Bayer's opinion, rigid symmetry and arbitrary geometry have no place in exhibition design. It is apparent from these observations that Bayer draws a sharp distinction between exhibition and display design—the latter, being capable of comprehension at a glance, presents no problems of development in time and can therefore be treated as a static object.

116

Models of two exhibitions: "Road to Victory" (above) and "Airways to Peace." Note that the exact size and position of all major elements are completely worked out at small scale.

continued

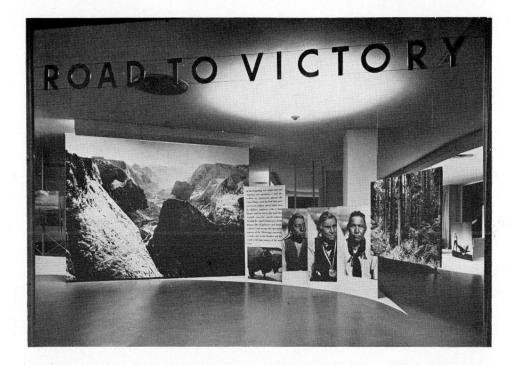

On these two pages are shown the entrances or "frontispieces" to four of Bayer's exhibitions. In each, the problem was the same: to reveal at first glance something of the nature and scope of the show inside. In the "Road to Victory" introduction, he used text (large enough to be read) and photographs indicating the emphasis on people and natural resources. The historical nature of the "Airways to Peace" exhibition is suggested with extreme directness by the juxtaposition of a modern plane and a drawing of Icarus. In neither of these two wartime shows did the designer find it necessary to resort to flags, banners, statues of liberty or any of the other overworked and frequently commercialized symbols.

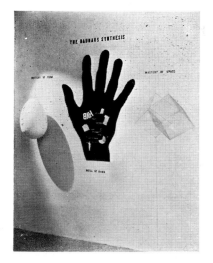

At left, entrance panel to the Bauhaus exhibition. Below, entrance to a show on modern art in advertising. Note how Bayer used his favorite tension lines here to draw in the visitor—and to neutralize the drab architecture.

Any traveling exhibit has two main requirements to fill: it must be capable of repeated erection and demounting without damage or loss of parts, and it must fit a variety of average spaces. This traveling student exhibit from the Chicago Institute of Design looks a bit optimistic on both counts. One gets the impression that erection might require something of a crew—and a well-briefed one at that—and it appears that a rather large, high room would be needed to take it. As a display, the show is neatly organized and the material is handsomely presented. Design credits belong to Robert Brownjohn and William Kessler, students at the time, who worked under the direction of Serge Chermayeff, then head of the school.

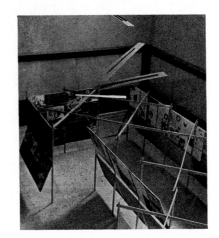

Most displays are forced to ignore, or try to cancel out, building backgrounds. Here, in the museum of the Contemporary Arts Association of Houston, Texas, architects MacKie and Kamrath designed a structure intended to facilitate the solving of exhibition problems. The building is designed rather like an industrial skylight—without the factory beneath it. The section is based on what appears to be a 30-60-degree triangle and thus provides two long walls (or ceilings) of different slopes. The one facing in the photograph is covered in corrugated material, some opaque and some translucent. It will be noted that that wall used for fabric display lends itself naturally to the "field of vision" type of arrangement developed by Herbert Bayer. Space of this kind has many advantages apart from its obvious economy: the feeling of complete enclosure created by the sloping surfaces is most pleasant, and where vertical panels are introduced into the scheme they count with unusual effectiveness. It would also be possible, in such an interior, to develop shows which do not rely on the surrounding walls at all except to take advantage of the extra ceiling height for special lighting, hanging displays, etc. Designers of the displays were Frank Dolejska and Robert Preusser.

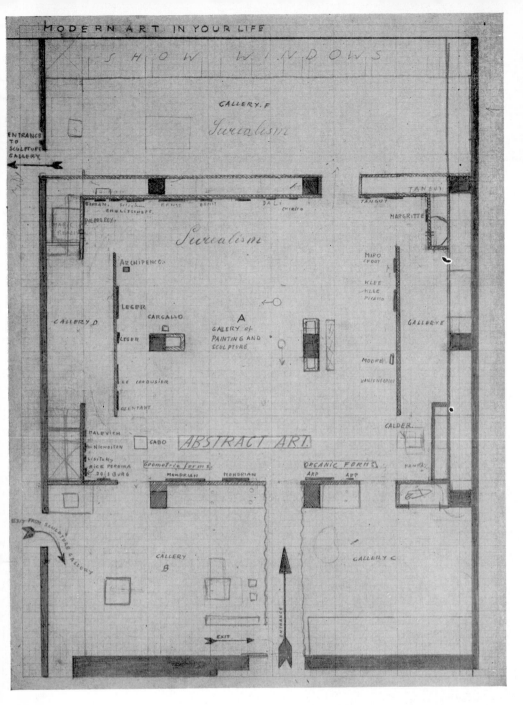

The plan shows a "ring" scheme centering around a large gallery in which painting and sculpture are shown. Great care was taken to relate the central exhibits with the rooms beyond. For instance, in the photograph directly above, one sees past the abstract paintings in the central gallery to a small architectural exhibit in which the buildings show a character similar to that of the paintings. In the same way, an opening in the wall dedicated to surrealist painting leads to the gallery in which applications of this approach are shown (lower photograph, facing page). Robert Goldwater collaborated with René d'Harnoncourt in the preparation of the exhibition and catalog.

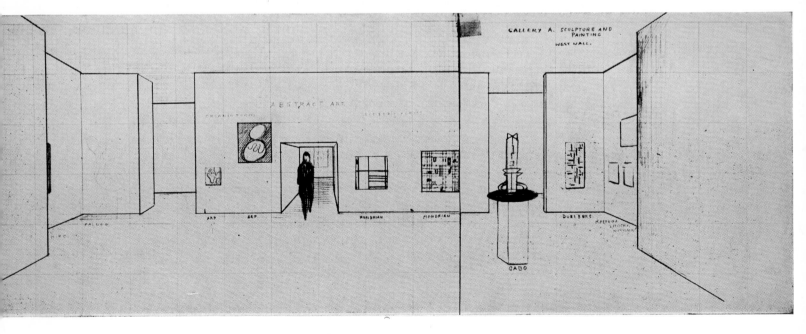

Right, low tunnel entrance to Gallery A. The visitor entered between semi-transparent screens through which he got glimpses of the displays in galleries B and C. Below, Gallery F.

"Modern Art in Your Life"

Some exhibitions are hard to design because of space problems, budget limitations, technical difficulties and the like; others encounter their main troubles in the subject matter itself. If René d'Harnoncourt found it difficult to put this show together ("Modern Art in Your Life," Museum of Modern Art, 1949) it would certainly have been for the latter reason. The idea seemed simple enough: show an interested public that the "fine" arts (painting and sculpture) and the applied arts grow out of the same common environment. It had been demonstrated over and over again that this fact was generally unknown or ignored: people who would not dream of giving house room to a painting by Mondrian would accept without the least concern a similar expression in the design of a box of Kleenex, a radio advertisement or a shop front. The problem was to present these various manifestations in some kind of juxtaposition which indicated the relationship but avoided oversimplification or vulgarization. Since people will inevitably draw their own conclusions when they see objects grouped in some physical relation to each other, it is possible that the problem was insoluble within the limits of a museum exhibit. The solution tried (plan, facing page) was to place the different kinds of contemporary painting and sculpture in a central gallery and to surround this gallery with a ring of other galleries in which architecture and the industrial arts were displayed. It is probable that this planning device was as good as any other, although it suggests that painting and sculpture are the major arts from which the others have developed, an implication which has frequently, but not always, proven true. The difficulty encountered in getting across a complex set of ideas suggests that in spite of the flexibility and dynamic quality of modern exhibition design, some concepts may be so involved that they strain the medium beyond its limits. One thing is evident from the various photographs: the surrealist method (above) can still beat anything else when it comes to putting on a dramatic display.

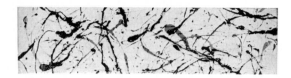

Arthur Drexler

Project for a Museum

The paintings of Jackson Pollock are huge, nervous doodles made in part by fastening the canvas to the floor and dribbling color on from above. The method—at least in Pollock's hands—results in rhythmic patterns with an extraordinary variety of textures. Like the work of Mark Rothko and Clifford Still, these pictures form something of a category of their own: too large to be hung as easel paintings, too devoid of objective content to be used as murals (most clients and patrons still expect murals in buildings to be pictures *of* something) these canvases have caused many to wonder what might be done with them. To Peter Blake, designer and friend of Pollock, there occurred the idea that they might serve admirably as the walls of an open pavilion. It was an excellent and appropriate idea: pictures of this type do not take kindly to framing and they do form screen walls in a completely natural manner. The museum which shelters these painting-walls is an entirely open affair with a plan in the manner of Mies van der Rohe and a roof designed to be entirely translucent. Wall-height mirrors are used in conjunction with the main painting at the center so that its pattern will appear to continue on indefinitely. The artist provided models of three sculptures, one of which is mounted in front of a semi-circular screen of perforated brass. This, incidentally, is the only wall in the pavilion which is not a painting. While the project is admittedly both extreme and theoretical, the thinking is constructive. There is no reason why painting could not come back into building at this scale and in this manner, and the work of Pollock seems ideally suited to the purpose.

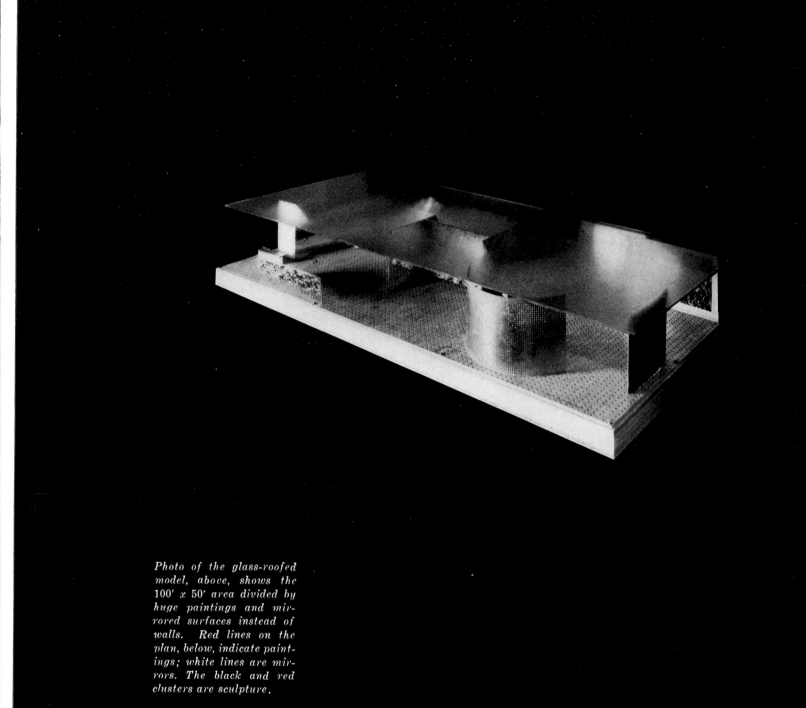

Photo of the glass-roofed model, above, shows the 100' x 50' area divided by huge paintings and mirrored surfaces instead of walls. Red lines on the plan, below, indicate paintings; white lines are mirrors. The black and red clusters are sculpture.

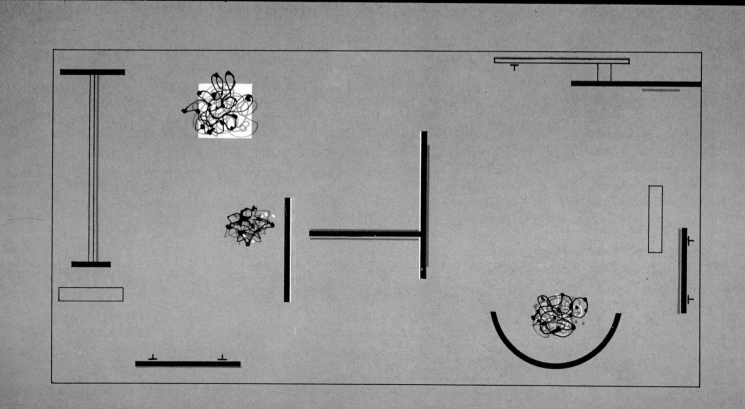

The paintings, sculpture and operable exhibits are brilliantly colored and they stand out sharply against the dark green walls. Sculptures on the pedestals include work by Flannagan, Zorach and Chaim Gross. The alligator is by Ruth Vollmer and the lucite giraffe (foreground) is by Toni Hughes. Victor d'Amico, director of the museum's educational program, designed the gallery.

Soichi Sunami

Soichi Sunami

Most museum shows are for adults, and it is generally taken for granted that the exhibits are not to be touched or manipulated. In this gallery at the Museum of Modern Art both rules are reversed: visitors are restricted to the ages between four and eight, and the restriction is enforced by a wire silhouette at the entrance (above) scaled approximately to the size of an eight year old. The unique feature of the gallery, however, is that the visitors are encouraged to handle the exhibits. Sculpture is set on pedestals low enough for the pieces to be touched as well as looked at. In addition there are a number of things designed to be operated, such as a juggler by Toni Hughes which is lever-controlled, a tightrope walker which goes across the room when a cord is pulled, and a color organ by Victor d'Amico which can be "played." The gallery is placed as an anteroom to an inner space where paper and paints are kept available for the use of the children. The design problem in such an exhibit is obviously a special one: displays at floor level have to be selected on the basis of toughness as well as esthetic merit, fragile art objects must be hung well out of reach. This explains the placing of objects as shown in the photograph at the right. The children's gallery has been a great success since its inception a number of years ago, and the idea has been adopted by other museums across the country. Those who suffered as children on "cultural" Sunday visits to museums where nothing was explained and everything was untouchable will have no trouble in understanding the popularity of this new approach.

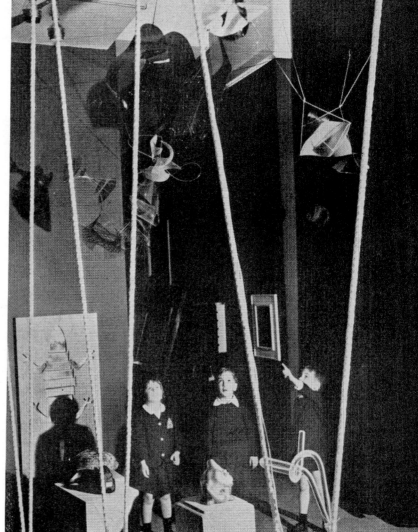

photo: courtesy of Monsanto Chemical Company

Gallery for Children

"Good Design": 1950

Carl Ullrich, inc.

Photos (top and left) Fran Byrne

The "Good Design" exhibitions jointly sponsored by the Museum of Modern Art and the Chicago Merchandise Mart have provided the occasion for an annual series of display designs which have been quite remarkable for their variety and excellence. These shows cover a broad range of products in the home furnishings field: major and small appliances, furniture, floor and wall coverings, fabrics, lamps, tableware and accessories. The entire program is under the direction of Edgar Kaufmann Jr., and selections are made twice a year from new merchandise in production by a three-man jury consisting of Mr. Kaufmann and two invited members.

The show is held in a large space—over five thousand square feet—in the Merchandise Mart, and each year it is completely done over by an appointed designer whose job it is not only to house the many hundreds of items in visible and appropriate settings, but to create in the exhibition as a whole a distinguished contemporary interior. By now, the entire "Good Design" program and its annual exhibitions (January in Chicago, and in the fall at the Museum of Modern Art in New York) have taken on something of the character of an institution, and the influence of the program has been widely felt. The Chicago exhibit is timed to coincide with the big furniture market in January, and since the Merchandise Mart is a major display center for manufacturers, the exhibit is visited by buyers from all over the country. Inevitably the choice of objects has influenced buyers and has helped them become more familiar with a kind of design which, only a few years back, was restricted to a small number of special retail shops. The publicity given the selected products, in both newspapers and magazines, has also had an important influence on consumer demand. Designers too have benefited greatly, either by having their work called to the attention of potential clients, or by gaining increased freedom in the creation of designs previously considered too radical for public acceptance. The meaning of these exhibitions, therefore, goes far beyond that of the average display interior.

The 1950 show, illustrated here, was the first of the series and was designed by Charles and Ray Eames who transformed the drab and anonymous space into a beautifully modeled and lighted interior. The focal point of the show, the "Hall of Light," (above and left) had a provocative display of objects of other periods: a 13th Century Madonna, a bentwood chair, a tailor's shears and so on. In spite of the great number of objects to be displayed, the space was handled so that it appeared open and uncluttered. Other details of the design are shown on the following page.

129

Space in the Merchandise Mart, as in most buildings of this type, is conspicuous for the number of beams, girders, air-conditioning ducts, pipes and sprinklers which criss-cross all over the ceilings. These familiar obstacles to the creation of a clean interior can be done away with by the simple—and very expensive—device of a hung ceiling, but it has been the policy in the "Good Design" show space to leave them exposed, facing each new designer with this challenge to his ingenuity. Some of the expedients tried by the Eames' are shown at the right. Ducts were converted into decorative elements with black paint and white stripes at the joints.

Consistent with this kind of articulation is the use of the Thru-Vue blind as a partition. The illustration at the right is very much in the same vein: the pipes serving the sprinkler system have been pressed into service for the support of clamp-on type spotlights. The wall in the background is covered with Chinese tea chest papers.

photos on this page: Charles Eames

The designers wanted the exhibit to be visible from the building corridor, and to get this effect quite a few feet of corridor wall were torn down. Instead of filling the gap with the customary sheets of plate glass the designers used folding gates, painted black, which serve as window, wall and entrance door.

At the right, another example of an open type of space divider. Here the idea of vertically hung strings, used in a great variety of forms in the doorways of bars in the countries around the Mediterranean and the Caribbean, has been interpreted in chain. Here an ancient device for letting the people in and keeping the flies out has been transformed into a highly decorative contemporary screen.

Carl Ullrich. inc.

"Good Design": 1951

The second of the Good Design shows was done by Finn Juhl, Danish architect and designer, who had just become known in this country for his beautifully detailed and finished wood furniture. Juhl had to work under the difficulty of not being able to see the space for which he was designing until he came over to supervise the actual construction. He also had the problem of not knowing precisely what objects were to be exhibited. This, incidentally, is a problem for all of the designers due to the necessity of preparing drawings for the space well in advance of the final selections made by the jury. Still another problem is created by a second selection of products in June: the exhibit must be sufficiently flexible to accommodate these mid-year additions without major changes.

In making his layout for the space, Finn Juhl took the option of charting an exact course for the visitor to follow (see plans on following page) and he used glass partitions, display tables set between columns (above) and other devices to route traffic in the desired direction. Juhl developed a quiet scheme, with pale colors and plenty of light as the background for the objects. To mark off the different sections of the show into distinct areas he varied floor coverings and ceiling treatments.

continued

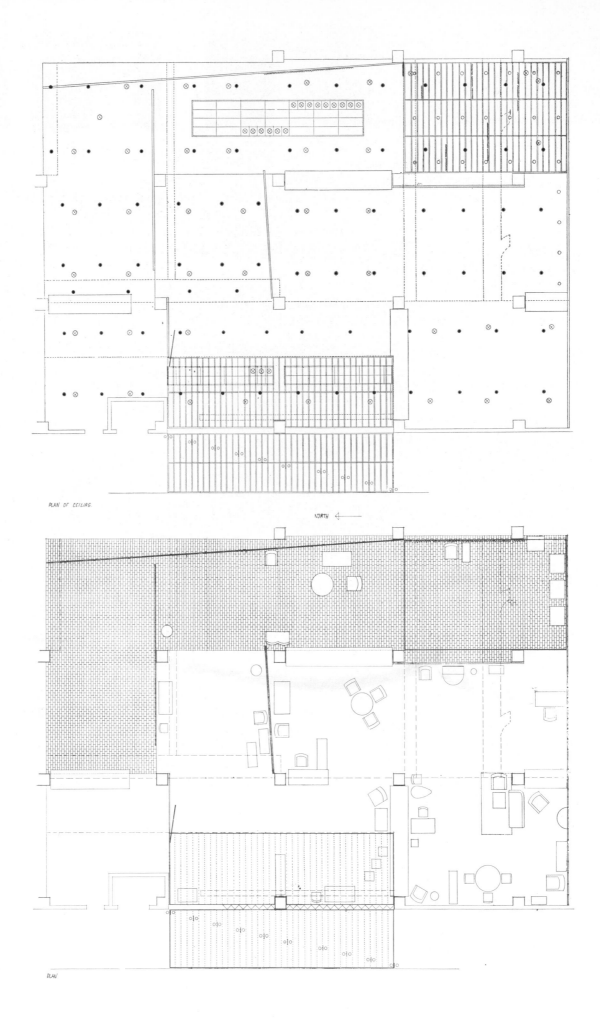

PLAN OF CEILING.

NORTH ←

PLAN

*Two views of the Finn Juhl design for the 1951 show. The photograph at the bottom was taken near the entrance, and it shows the enormous plate glass screen (light green in color) beyond which the visitor had to pass. The ceiling (in spite of the pipes, ducts, etc.) is brightly illuminated in most areas, and the bulk of the down lighting is handled by exposed reflector lamps. As in most of these exhibits, furniture is scattered through the entire area, while smaller objects, such as china, silver and accessories are grouped on special display tables and counters. Fabrics are grouped against the wall. As shown here the fabrics are easily viewed and compared, but the continuous hanging, made up of so many different weights and textures of materials, leaves something to be desired from the viewpoint of display technique. The upper photograph has in the foreground one of the long display tables given double use as a counter and as a barrier. Juhl's procedure in hanging the table between two columns is admirable: it not only leaves the floor entirely free, but the elimination of legs also removes **any possibility of confusing a display unit with the furniture on exhibit.***

It might well be imagined that with each succeeding year the job of the designer—with so many first-rate solutions already before him—would become increasingly difficult. Perhaps the difficulty has increased, but the "Good Design" exhibitions for both 1952 and 1953 set new highs in treatments for the space. The 1952 show, designed by Paul Rudolph, was an extraordinarily sensitive and imaginative solution. In this exhibition, Rudolph (a young architect in practice in Sarasota, known only for his distinguished houses) revealed an unexpected flair for the dramatic. If one considers the materials used, the show is seen to consist of almost nothing: plastic cord, sprayed Cocoon, eggcrate light baffles and other devices of extreme transparency or fragility; yet the result surpassed both its predecessors in its impact. The reason lay almost entirely in the masterly use of light. Rudolph's own statement does much to reveal the thinking behind this project:

"The fundamental idea behind the exhibition installation is to provide psychological contrasts. This is accomplished by arranging constricted spaces so that they are in juxtaposition to freely flowing spaces with distant vistas. In addition, brightly illuminated areas penetrate into fields less brightly lighted. Psychologically this should mean that the visitor becomes less tired on his tour through the exhibition. A comparison may be made with the experience of seeing the sun disappear behind a cloud only to shine brightly again, which makes us feel exhilarated.

"There is a prescribed route to follow, although there are many bypasses. Opaque and translucent screen walls made of plastic cords, Cocoon (a plastic spray developed by the Armed Forces to preserve their materiel), woven cane, are so arranged that one can compare visually an item seen earlier with one just coming into view.

"The color of the exhibits is emphasized by keeping all tones on backgrounds, floors and ceilings in a range from white through black, accented only by gold on two faces of the columns."

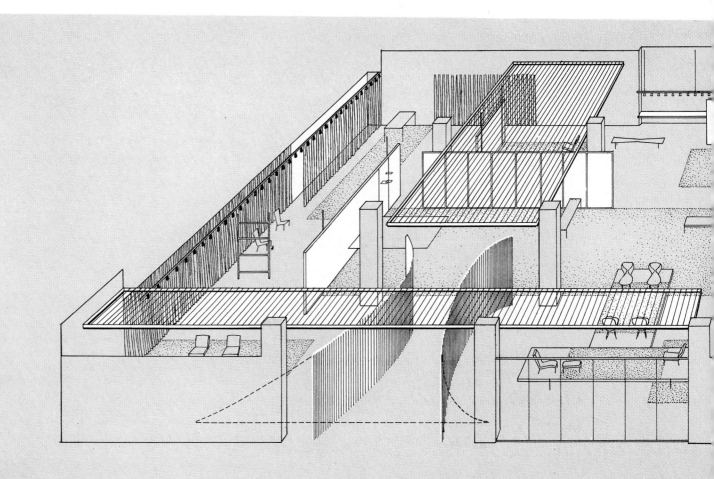

Carl Ullrich, inc.

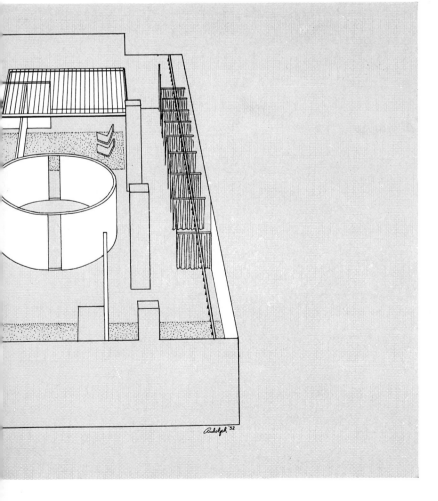

Mr. Rudolph's drawing at the left gives a
good picture of the general scheme of the
exhibition, showing the curved screens at
the entrance, the "cocoon" sprayed wall facing the main axis, the circular room used
as an office and the overhead lighting grids.
The last, incidentally, were one of the
really inspired ideas of the entire exhibit:
painted a charcoal gray and illuminated in
a spotty rather than an even manner, they
created a series of pools of light which
were wonderfully effective. For the success
of the lighting, Richard Kelly should be
credited for his collaboration as lighting
consultant. The photograph directly above
is a view from the entrance and illustrates
clearly the combination of a sense of enclosure and transparency described in Mr.
Rudolph's statement on the opposite page.
What is particularly revealing about this
design is its demonstration of the value of
certain techniques, such as the use of
stretched cord, to create a real sense of
separation and enclosure with a negligible
weight and quantity of actual material.

continued

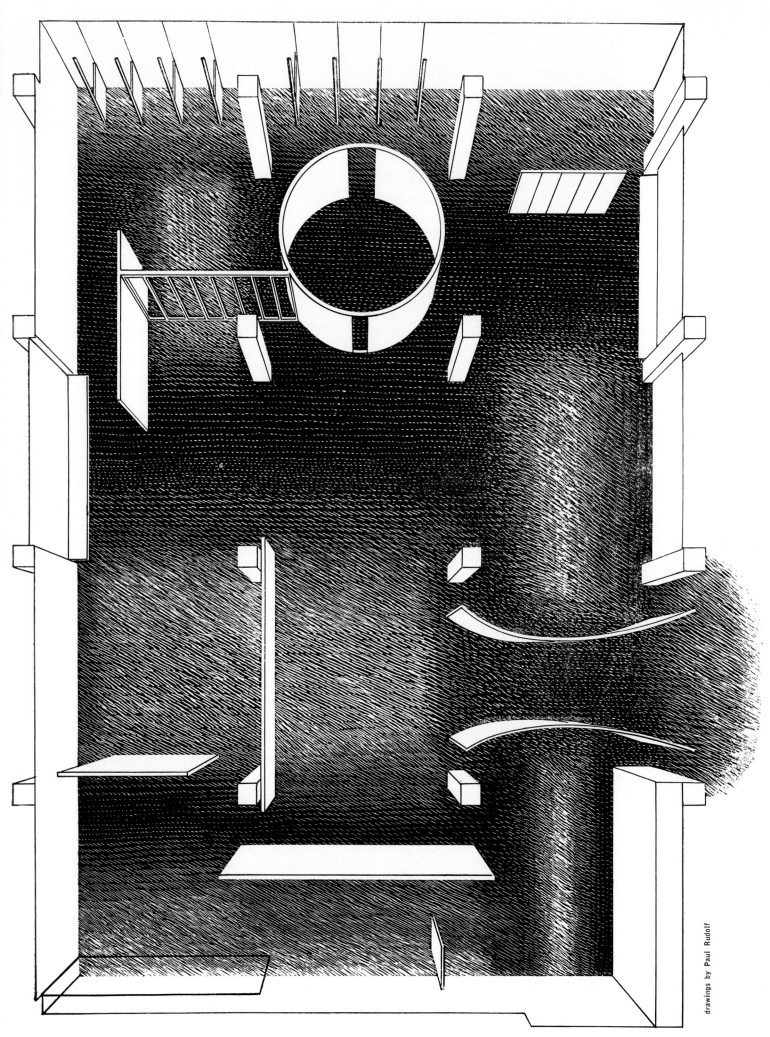

drawings by Paul Rudolf

all photographs by Carl Ullrich Inc., except where otherwise noted.

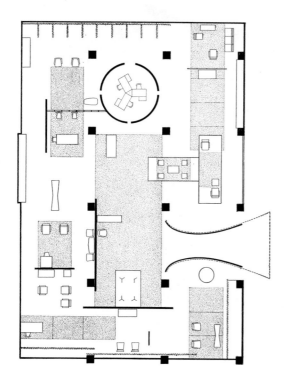

Studied in conjunction with each other, the plan and isometric drawing show the way in which solids (and semi-solids) have been employed to define and reveal the quality of the open space. The solid cylinder has three slits and a door. It was the intention of the designer to install a periscope inside for providing other views of the exhibition. Shortly after the opening, however, the space was taken over for use as an office and the cylinder's interior lost all of its meaning and value as part of the show. As in former exhibits, furniture was distributed fairly generally throughout the space. Fortunately it was possible, through this scattering, to keep individual furniture clusters, as above, fairly sparse and loosely related so that each piece could be viewed without confusion. In this photograph one can also enjoy the skillful and inconspicuous handling of the lighting.

continued

Illustrations at the upper right and bottom left provide two views of the fabric displays. The designer separated prints from textured materials by putting the former on the wall, the latter on low racks. Below, chairs in string and metal mesh are displayed against a screen of cane.

What color is to be found in the exhibit is always in the objects themselves since backgrounds are restricted to black, white, gray, gold and the color of natural fiber.

Many kinds of openwork screens were used. Below, a detail of metal mesh screening sprayed with "cocoon" and then punched out in a pattern of small open squares.

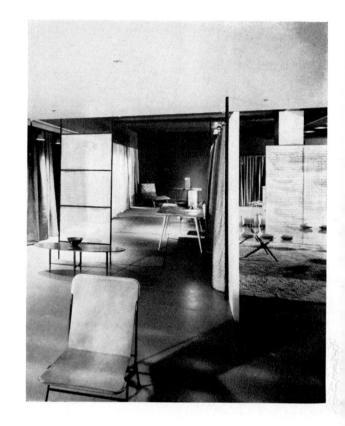

Below, one of the displays of smaller objects. Note how rich an effect is created by the display on a white counter set against a dark wall of perforated board. Note, too, how the lighting has been placed so that there is a cutoff about a foot or two above the counter.

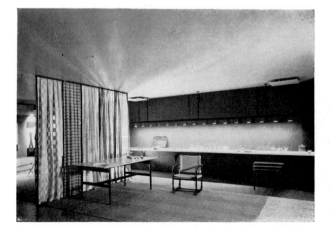

A divider made by hanging fabrics within a metal frame which extends the full height from floor to ceiling. In the background, another display shelf for glassware and accessories, illuminated by a row of small downlights.

"Good Design": 1952
Museum of Modern Art, New York

In addition to having the responsibility for the big show in Chicago, each designer also has to do a smaller exhibit at the Museum of Modern Art in the fall. Both the size and nature of the space is very different. The Merchandise Mart provides a large area, similar to that of a loft building in character, with no natural light. The Museum space is very much smaller, quite finished in appearance, and equipped with a continuous wall of glass fronting on the museum's garden. The designer's job, therefore, is to take into account these changed circumstances and, in the smaller space, to duplicate the spirit rather than the detail of the Chicago show. The photographs on these two pages show Paul Rudolph's solution. While very different in appearance, the same general ideas are in evidence: the lighting for demarcation of areas and for establishing contrasts, the use of achromatic backgrounds to allow the color in the products to register, the use of perforated screens, the establishment of solids which penetrate the space. Because of the abundance of natural daylight, the lighting scheme is inevitably keyed higher than it was in Chicago.

photos: Alexandre Georges

The approach to lighting and layout was the same for the museum show as it was for the mart, but interpreted with different materials. Here, areas of light were diffused by panels of Fiberglas hung in front of windows or below overhead lamps. Again, there was the strong contrast between spot lighting and whole illuminated ceilings which also served to define given display areas. At one end of the space, a round free-standing enclosure was made of fabric lengths hung around a circular track. The screen at entrance below, is of shaped cardboard held between wood uprights, and is different from, but reminiscent of, the strung and perforated screens invented for the Chicago show.

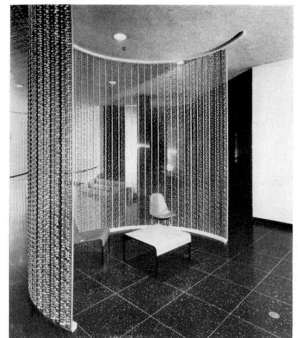

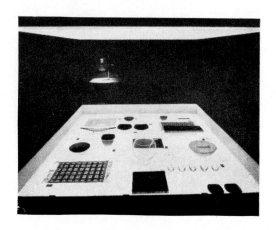

The handling of fabrics in Alexander Girard's 1953 Good Design show was by far the most successful and imaginative of any. It is standard procedure to "drape" drapery fabrics to give some illusion of reality, but in an exhibition this tends to rather sloppy and confused effects. Girard's solution was to stretch the fabrics on panels and to set the panels both vertically and horizontally.

Examples of the backlighting technique used throughout the exhibit. At the left, a sheet of translucent Styrofoam is set as a table about one foot off the floor, on top of a box filled with lights, and forms a brilliantly glowing base for the display of tableware. Other examples of the technique appear below and on the opposite page.

Carl Ullrich, inc.

"Good Design": 1953

The most recent of the Good Design shows, designed by Alexander Girard, is also in many ways the most dramatic. In essence it is also the one which can be described as the most simple although the simplicity is somewhat deceptive. This show is one with no backgrounds: all walls and the ceiling have been painted black, so that they disappear; within this black envelope the exhibits appear, set on, against or into glowing surfaces of light. The device was used in a limited way by Max Bill in one of the Triennale exhibits (page 76) but it is doubtful if anyone has carried the technique to this limit before. Through the entire exhibition there is the effect of glowing light in a surrounding of blackness, but there is no immediately obvious source of the light, nor does the light have any visible direction. A beautiful example of what can be achieved with this approach is shown above, in the bright, compartmented wall which both permeates the exhibited objects with lights, and silhouettes them. To achieve this effect the designer used not only black paint where it would do the most good, but he pasted dark-toned velvet flock paper on inner partitions, covered large sections of floor with a black vinyl-impregnated cork, and then used his translucent plastic panels to gain a maximum effect. From the viewpoint of proper merchandise display this whole approach might perhaps be questioned; but when it is recalled that the "Good Design" shows are designed to highlight the best in production of things for the home, and that their function is not so much to sell as to shock into awareness those who come to see, the Girard solution seems admirably calculated to do precisely this.

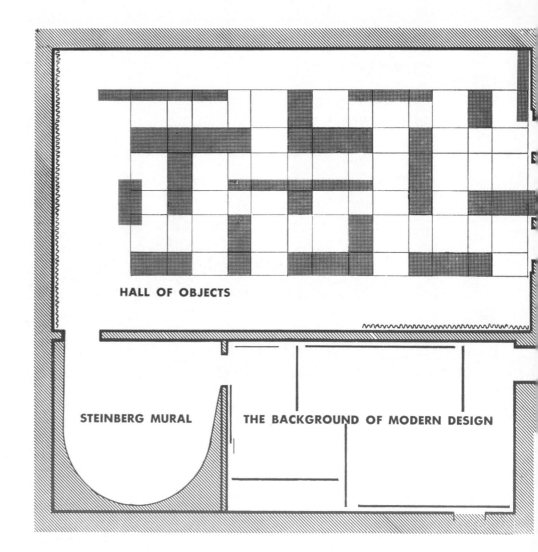

HALL OF OBJECTS

STEINBERG MURAL   THE BACKGROUND OF MODERN DESIGN

This exhibition, the largest of its kind ever held, was shown at the Detroit Institute of Arts in 1949 under the sponsorship of the J. L. Hudson Company. Whether this august and financially replete institution knew what it was getting in for when it put itself into the hands of Alexander Girard is entirely a matter of conjecture. What is a matter of fact is that months after the rest of the country had heard about it, the Hudson store's own buyers finally learned that their company had sponsored the most complete show of contemporary furniture and household accessories that had ever been held anywhere. But it is not the purpose of this book to dwell upon the eccentricities of buyers or the vagaries of the retail merchandising business.

"For Modern Living", among other things, marked the emergence to national recognition of Alexander Girard as one of the country's most brilliantly imaginative and superlatively competent designers. Lost for more years than anyone can remember in a golden haystack known as Grosse Pointe, one of the stuffier of the nation's suburban communities, Girard suddenly came forward with a statement of what a major exhibition should be which has not yet been excelled—or, for that matter, matched. It was the first full-scale treatment of the "good design" theme so ably handled by the designers shown on the preceding pages.

Girard's exhibition, held in the pseudo-Renaissance halls of the Detroit museum, completely transformed the interior, introduced the full range of contemporary display techniques and demonstrated with over-abundant clarity the existence of good modern furniture and accessories. The show took the visitor through a hall of mirrors (in the best amusement-park manner), past an historical exhibit (photo, opposite page), up to an enormous Steinberg mural, through the hall of objects, into a multi-level display of rooms and gardens. Other photographs will be found on the following pages.

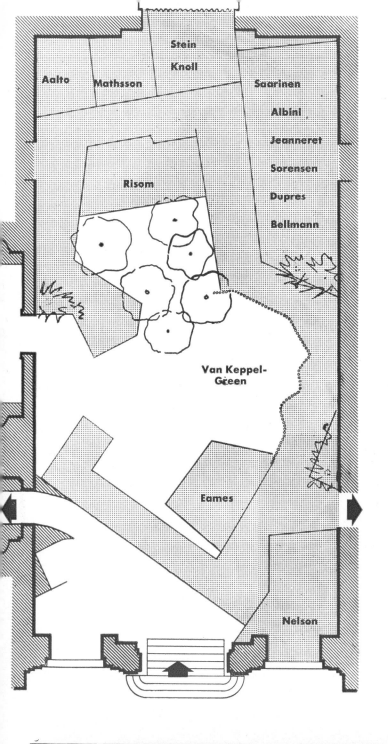

Below, three of the display rooms by (top to bottom) Alvar Aalto, Florence Knoll and Jens Risom. Other rooms, and part of the garden were shown on pp. 64 to 67.

Elmer L. Astleford

photos: Elmer L. Astleford

The display in the Great Hall was devoted to specially designed rooms and a garden fitted out with full-scale trees. When it is realized that this was a traditional museum central hall, filled with Renaissance architectural details and massive sculptures, the completeness of the transformation will be more apparent.

The Steinberg mural commented in the inimitable Steinberg fashion on modern life, surroundings and design. Above, a fragment from the mural devoted to the great national pastime of moving. At right, a detail of the Hall of Objects, filled with Unistrut structures of stainless steel which support an immense variety of shelves, objects and display backgrounds. The lighting, it will be observed, was handled in the same spirit as the structure. As in all of Girard's exhibit designs, the show was characterized by a fully developed idea carried out in great style and with many dramatic shifts in tempo. For an example of some of the contrasts provided, compare the structural approach to the display of objects with the small photograph at top right, where trees, garden furniture and concealed lighting set the mood for the displays in the Great Hall. The illustration on the opposite page gives a rather inadequate glimpse of the hall display in course of construction but it does show the emphasis on the use of changing levels.

Transportation Exhibit, Milan: 1948

International expositions have periodically left behind them structures of outstanding value: to mention only two, the Eiffel Tower and the Crystal Palace. Each was in its way prophetic; revealing possibilities in construction not yet realized. This railroad shed at the 1948 transportation exhibition is in the same general category as both, though less conspicuously ambitious than either. Here, as in the earlier structures mentioned, the theme is lightness. The shed is a flat roof set in a simple incline, part solid and part open trellis, supported by a series of inclined masts and cables in tension. In the spirit of a temporary exhibit, the masts are constructed of the same tubular metal parts used for building scaffoldings and rise out of a platform made of wood slats. The whole structure is virtually perfect for its purpose: it is obviously not permanent, it has the fresh gaiety one associates with the best fair designs, it is daring in a way workaday buildings cannot hope to match, it is bold in scale, and it stands as a fitting symbol of the spirit which has animated Italian designers since the war. The railroad trains sheltered by the shed are quite up to the design level set by the structure. Designer: Renzo Zavenella.

Seen in the photograph directly above, and in silhouette through the trellis roof at the left, is the exhibition tower which rises up like something constructed with a child's giant erector set. Other illustrations are shown on the following page.

Above, the exhibition tower; and below, the train for which the railroad shed was designed. Both are good examples of post-war Italy's ability to improvise. The tower is made of standard scaffolding parts —a sensible and appropriate use of materials in a country which had barely recovered from the worst of its war damage. The train had been bombed, and in its reconstruction the designer took advantage of the opportunity to incorporate a dome and to redesign and recondition the entire car.

Doisneau

The International Exposition of City Planning and Housing, Paris: 1949

The more one looks at exhibitions, the more evident it seems that prizes never go to the faint of heart. Here, for instance, is a large show devoted to city planning and housing. It was held inside the Grand Palais, an exhibition hall constructed largely of glass and considered suitable for generations for the housing of displays of virtually every description. In this case the designer entirely ignored the existing structure—much like Alexander Girard with his "For Modern Living" (p. 147)—and put up his own building inside the building. The resulting structure, whether one likes it or not, definitely sets its own scale and mood and depends on the shell above only to keep out the rain. Architect: André Hermant.

151

continued

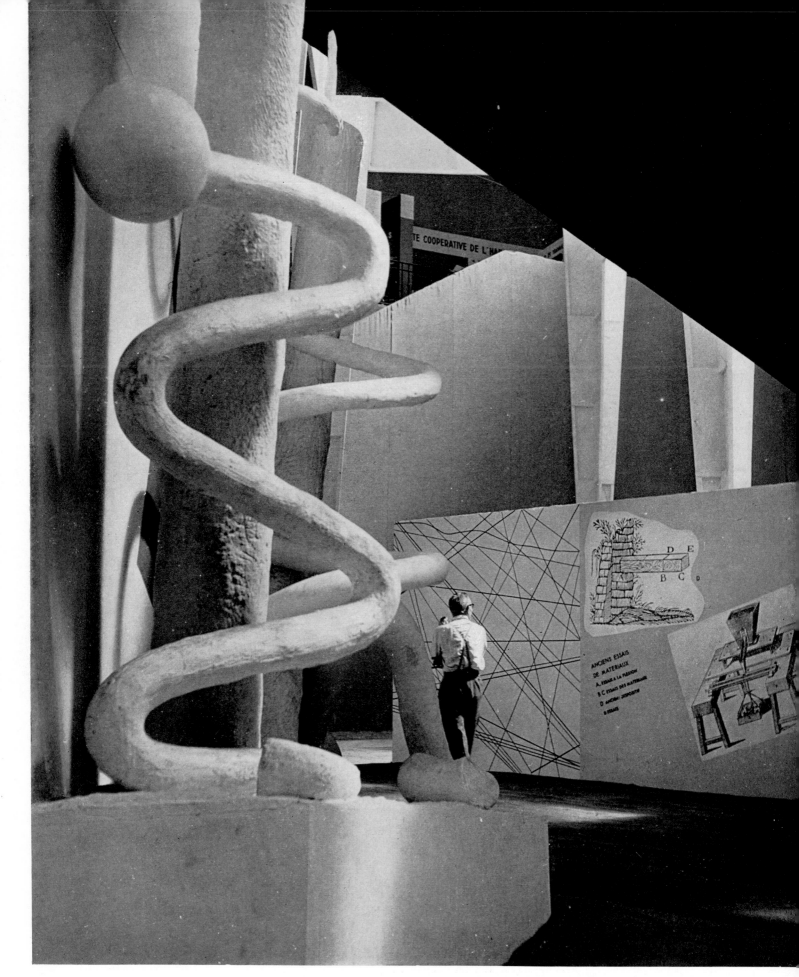

Doisneau

The scale of the planning exhibition in the Grand Palais is well shown in this photograph of the entrance to the section devoted to scientific research in materials and construction methods. The sculpture by Gin is well calculated to call attention to the size of the display as a whole. This part of the exposition was designed by André Bouxin.

The French section on city planning, designed by Robert Auzelle in collaboration with architects Faraut and Ghiula-mila, is more interesting as display than as city planning.

Throughout the exposition, three-dimensional models were used extensively. Right, a panel in the research section by Bouxin and Gin indicating the relative positions of the various research organizations. Below, a relief plan of an urban unit. The device is less expensive than a model but far more effective than a flat map.

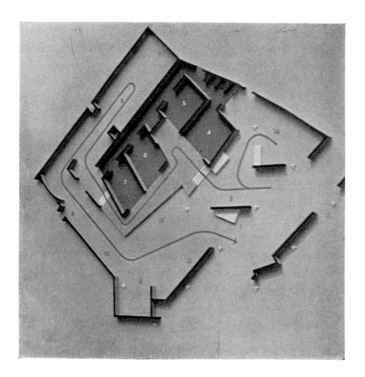

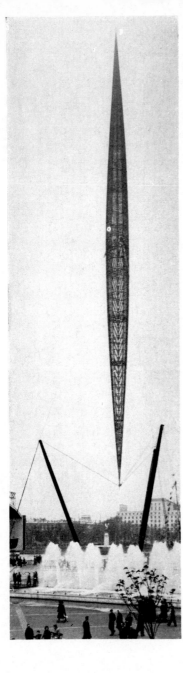

The "Skylon," designed by Philip Powell and Hidalgo Moya, comes straight out of science fiction. The huge toothpick shape floats without apparent weight over a circular fountain whose form suggests the ring of smoke from the exhaust of a rocket. The spectacular quality of the design, its obvious lack of practical use and its completely temporary look are all superlatively appropriate in the context of a great exhibition.

The Festival of Britain: 1951

"The Festival of Britain," writes the *Architectural Review* of London, "was conceived at a moment when the temperature chart of British history, which throughout recorded time has fluctuated violently between fever heat and absolute zero, could be seen by the whole world to register several degrees below normal. There was no reason—no excuse even—for holding another Great Exhibition, except those provided by memories of the Prince Consort's courage and enterprise a hundred years before and Paxton's engineering genius."

The "excuse" to which the *Review* refers was the Great Exhibition of 1851, and it was the Crystal Palace built for that exhibition which remained for nearly a hundred years as the monument to Paxton's genius. In planning the 1951 Festival of Britain as a centennial celebration, the architects and designers had a different site, a very different national climate (Britain was in a state of near-collapse after the war and its empire was crumbling to bits) and a whole new world of technology. As a goal to shoot at, there was the memory of the Crystal Palace, still an unmatched masterpiece of exhibition architecture.

The great contribution of the Festival was in its plan—the first great exhibition to depart from the formal, symmetrical design which had held sway since the Renaissance. Instead, the layout of the exhibition was like the planning for a modern city center. The buildings which housed the displays, or were themselves displays, did not come up to the standards set in the 19th Century by the Crystal Palace or Eiffel Tower, but they showed great fertility of ideas and a strong sense of what was essentially contemporary. The Dome of Discovery, for instance, was a circular shed 365 feet in diameter with a saucer-like roof of aluminum supported on struts of tubular steel. Designed by Ralph Tubbs, the structure was the largest at the fair and far more successful in conveying its bold and simple idea outside than inside. Like the rather interplanetary "Skylon" above, it did express the experimental approach typical of the Festival's structures and plan.

continued

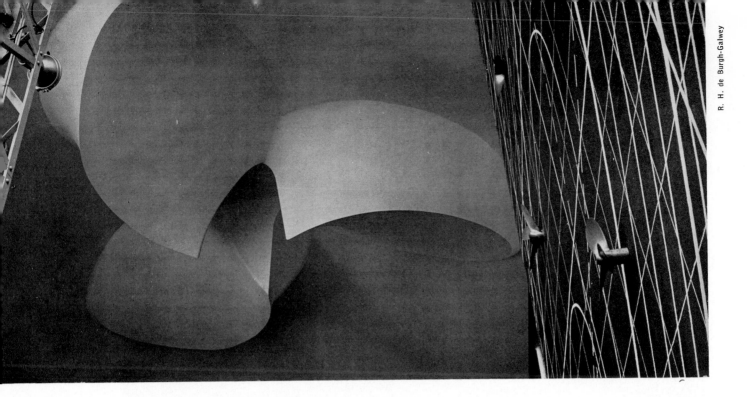

A detail which demonstrates the frequent mixtures of styles seen through the exhibition. Here large concrete forms are used in juxtaposition with cages of glass and steel.

"Sea and Ships"

Like any other fair exhibition, the Festival of Britain housed its displays in buildings. A major exception, however, was the section designated "Sea and Ships" in which a majority of the displays *were* the buildings. Located on the edge of the river, this area contained ships in model, full-size parts of ships, diving and fishing gear, marine objects and equipment of all descriptions. Parts of the display were in the open and others were under cover. The general idea was an inspired one for it permitted the designers to introduce among the more conventional building shapes a variety of large marine forms which added interest and a feeling of gaiety. Designer: Basil Spence and Partners.

The "Lion and the Unicorn" pavilion was perhaps the most obviously British in its use of the contemporary idiom—and possibly just for that reason, one of the most popular. The structure was designed to symbolize the British character and tradition and contained judges' robes, law books, mottoes, filigree decorations and plaster doves under the lamella arch timber ceiling. The building was constructed as a steel frame box with two solid walls and two walls of glass. As a display, the interior is most interesting for the manner in which large historical objects (e.g. the lectern in the photograph at the right) have been combined with modern display cases and other elements to create a dignified, harmonious and lively effect. R. D. Russell and R. Y. Goodden, designers.

continued

Millar & Harris

The Royal Festival Hall is not display architecture, properly speaking. It was constructed as the only permanent structure in the exhibition and will become the core of a future development of the Thames South Bank. This large auditorium is significant on two counts: it is the first important public building in England to be designed as a contemporary building (a circumstance which can be traced directly to the influence of the exhibition of which it was a part) and in the second place, it again points up the role of big fairs in city redevelopment. Architect: Robert Matthew with J. L. Martin, Edwin Williams and Peter Moro.

The photograph above shows one of the main stairways in the Royal Festival Hall, a spiral of concrete with wood treads. Again the influence of the exhibition on a normally formal and uninspired type of civic building is clearly in evidence.

Council of Industrial Design

Thames-Side Restaurant

The Festival restaurants were carefully placed to take advantage of views of the city and the river. The one shown here was set up as both a boardwalk and cafe. The treatment shows a definite leaning to the nautical style, with a deck-type railing, red and white striped awning, and open-joint flooring. The use of a secondary railing in conjunction with the individual table lamps is an orderly and agreeable solution to a lighting problem which never seems to get solved in most eating places. Architects: Fry, Drew and Partners with Neville Ward and Frank Austin.

Lucio Fontana's great twisted loops of white neon tubing
hang above the main stairway in the entrance lobby of the Palazzo dell'Arte.
Architect: Luciano Baldessari; Marcello Grisotti, collaborator.
The fresco is by Bruno Cassinari.

The official symbol of the Triennale is shown at the right. It is a representation of some of the tools of the artist and the craftsman.

The Ninth Triennale, Milan: 1951

The Triennale (short Italian for The Triennial International Exposition of Modern and Decorative and Industrial Art and Modern Architecture) is held in Milan's Palazzo dell'Arte and surrounding park from May through October. It is a unique exposition in its size, scope and quality; and, since Italy's emergence after the war as a major center of creative activity in the arts, it has been watched with extreme interest by designers everywhere. One important element in the work of the Italians is responsible for this interest: its remarkable range and variety. Unlike the designers in, say, Sweden or Switzerland, the Italians have not clustered in a single, easily identified school. Their work includes the functional, the romantic and the prankish. Painting and sculpture range from abstraction to surrealism. The architects have let themselves be influenced by Wright as well as Le Corbusier, by the work of their own Renaissance, by such painters as Giorgio de Chirico. If there is an Italian school as such today, it is certainly the least hampered by dogma and the least inhibited in the world. The Triennale dates back to 1923, when it was held at Monza, and to 1933, when its permanent quarters were shifted to Milan. The plan of its main exhibition building (a not particularly distinguished structure) is shown overleaf. Its main virtue lies in the existence of a series of big, unencumbered spaces which are unbelievably transformed every three years by the appointed designers of the various sections. The show is given a major section in this book because its best exhibits represent an unequalled performance in the art of display. This art, incidentally, comprises more than the clever arrangement of exhibition interiors. Display means the display of *something,* and it must have as its object: instruction, entertainment or preferably both. The excellence of so much of the Italian work lies in the fact that no matter how dazzling the technique, the original objective of lucid exposition is never lost sight of. A relevant example is to be found in the neon lighting unit on the facing page. The designer took cognizance of two facts: (a) the hall needed illumination and (b) glass tubing can be bent. He came up with an answer which graphically communicated the gaiety and excitement of the show while providing the light needed as well. To do this is not quite as easy as it may look after the fact—it requires freedom, imagination and sensitivity, and Italy's contemporary designers are well supplied with all three.

continued

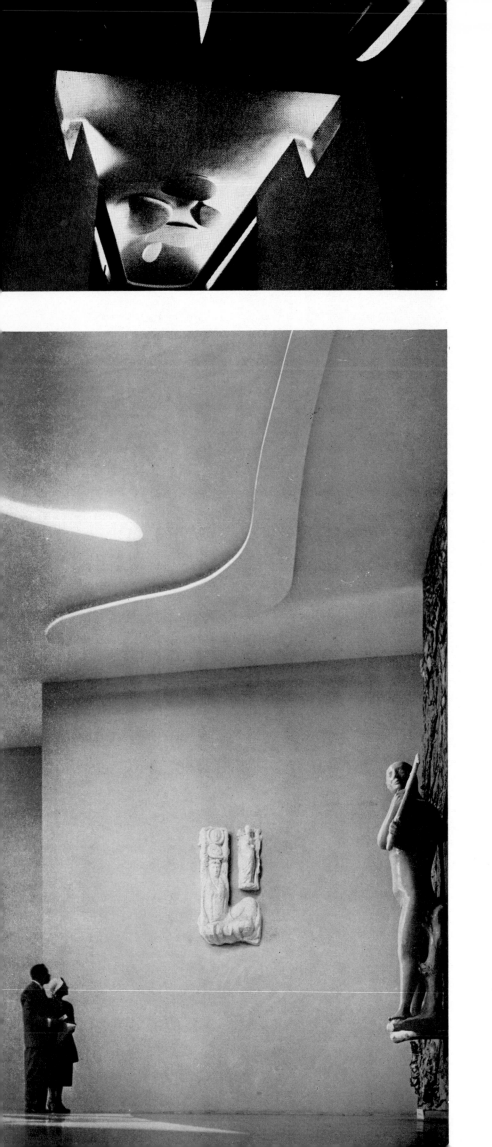

Both the plan (1) and the photographs suggest the sweep and scale of the treatment of the entrance to the exhibition. From the outer doors of the Palazzo dell'Arte a corridor with converging walls leads into an oval hall. Setting the walls up in this way greatly increases the apparent perspective, and hence the dramatic effect of the entrance. At the end of this path (2) is the great stair hall (see photographs on pp. 160 and 177) with its swirls of neon tubing.

All of these spaces are walled in with panels of various descriptions—curved, flat, overlapping, tilted—all painted in tones of gray. The floor is black linoleum with brilliant inlays as designed by Attilio Rossi. Lighting is occasionally recessed, but mainly located in troughs, and its effects are periodically heightened by the use of sculpture by Umberto Milani, as in the upper illustration. The effect of all these related spaces is light and alive, dramatic but yet subdued in relation to the exhibits proper. This kind of interior, where there is nothing in the way of "subject matter" to use for guidance, is perhaps the most difficult of all problems for the display designer.

continued

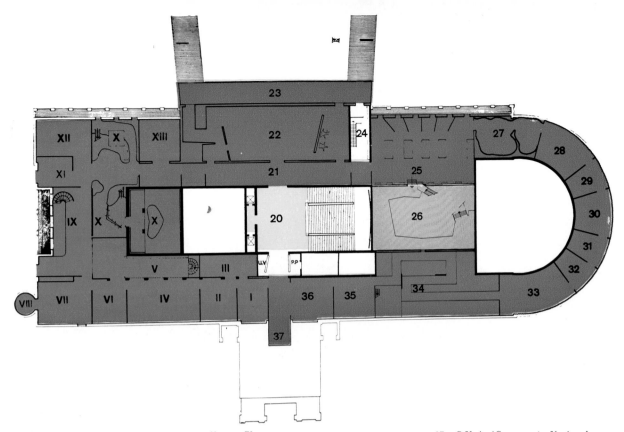

Ground Floor

1   Entrance
2   Lobby
3   The QT8 Project (Experimental Quarter)
4   A History of Modern Architecture
5   Architecture, Measure of Man
6   City Planning
7   The Dwelling
8   Industrial Design
9   Temporary Architecture
10   Theaters
11   Industry and Commerce
12   Schools
13   Hospitals
14   Hotels
15   Sports
16   Transportation
17   Advertising and Graphic Design
18   Spontaneous Architecture
19   In Memoriam

Upper Floor

20   Stairway and Lobby
21   The Literature of Design
22   The Door of the Duomo
23   Glassware
24   Lighting
25   Ceramics
26   The Italian Chair Through *The Ages*
27   Plastics
28   Metals
29   Gold- Silverware, Jewelry
30   Leather
31   Straw, Reeds and Wicker
32   Lace and Embroidery
33   Textiles
34   Furniture
35   State Art Institutes and Schools
36   E.N.A.P.I. (Ente Nazionale Artigianate Piccole Industrie—National Society of Small Handicrafts Industries)
37   C.N.A. (Compagnia Nazionale Artigiana—National Handicrafts Company)

Foreign Exhibitions (upper floor)

I   Britain
II   Spain
III Austria
IV Finland
V   West Germany
VI Netherlands
VII Sweden
VIII Orrefors glassware
IX Belgium
X   France
XI Robin Day
XII Denmark
XIII Switzerland
     uvv sales office
     p p post office

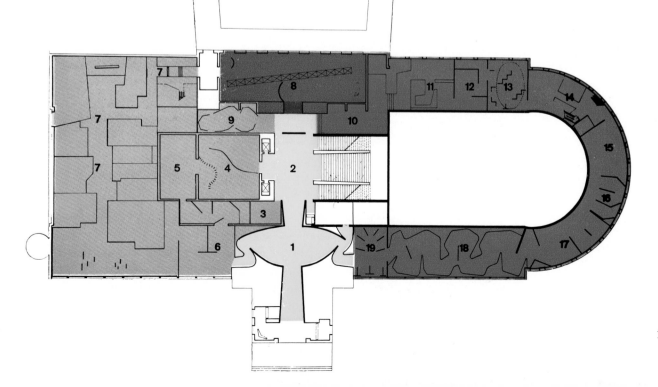

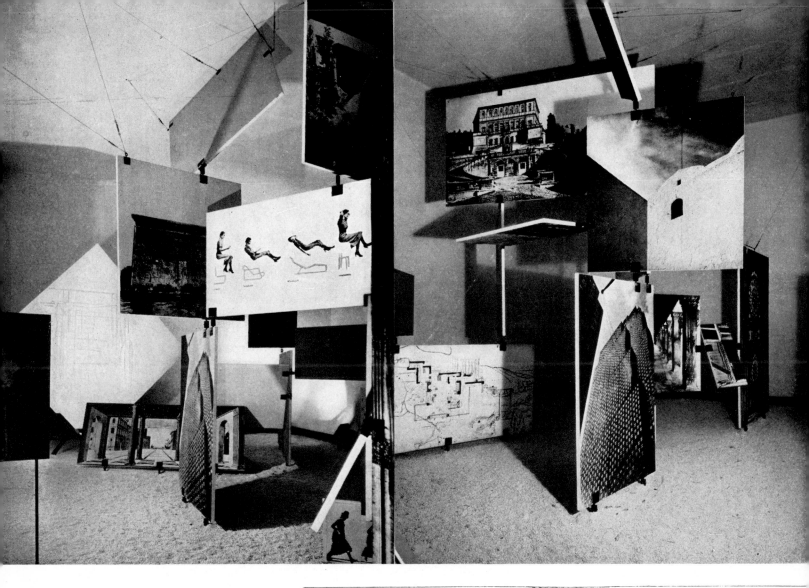

"Architecture, The Measure of Man"

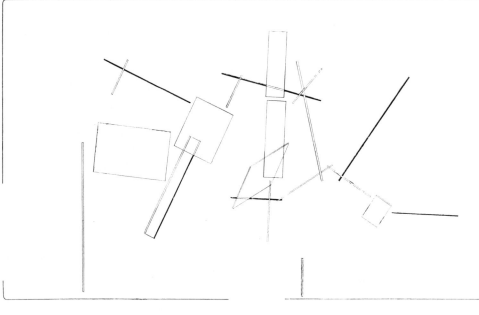

The theme of this section is that while man's physical dimensions and requirements have remained relatively the same through the ages, his spiritual dimensions and technical capacities have not. It is these developments which are reflected in the history of architecture. To communicate this idea Ernesto Rogers, with Vittorio Gregotti and Luigi Stoppino as collaborators, created an all-white space—including the gravel which serves as the floor—and installed in an apparently aimless manner a series of panels with photographs. Support is provided by both floor and ceiling. Both the display idea and its execution are brilliant—there has probably never been a better exhibit with only flat panels as its design material.

Publicity Section

The Triennale was full of sections each of which stood out as a model of its kind. In the Publicity exhibit, symbolized by a megaphone, the designers took one of the standard high-ceilinged rooms and, without architectural modification, converted it into a brassy, agitated display perfectly suggestive of its subject matter, and of the ulcer-ridden professions which create it. Every device introduced was used towards this end—the jagged canopies, the slatted ceiling and truncated panels. Woven through this highly charged background is the exhibit material which pictures the field of advertising and publicity (this is what the "ap" on the megaphone stands for) and includes outstanding examples of magazine covers, posters, advertisements and printing techniques. Architects: Erberto Carboni and Dino Villani.

continued

Sports Section

The section set aside for design in sports is a beautiful example of what can happen when the shapes of the objects permit the designer to throw away virtually all of the customary display props and equipment. This exhibit uses a shelf and a few stands, a few wire dummies for costumes and uniforms, and that is about all—everything else is the material on display: the hung shell, the pitched tent, the stretched sails. Architects: Vittoriano Viganò and Enrico Freyrie; sculptor: Umberto Milani; painters; Roberto Crippa and Gianni Dova.

continued **167**

Winding around the upper floors of the Palazzo dell'Arte there was an extensive series of spaces given over to the display of work done in particular materials (see plan, page 163). These included glass (pages 77, 176), ceramics, plastics, designs in gold and silver, jewelry (page 82), leather, straw, reeds and wicker, lace and embroidery, printed and woven textiles. It was in these sections that the extraordinary creative ferment which has been going on in Italy since the war was most fully revealed, for the exhibits made it clear that this is not an isolated expression on the part of a few gifted individuals, but a movement involving all of the design professions, and most of the arts and crafts. Because of the nature of the space and the display requirements of the products, these sections were not the most exciting of the exhibition designs (by contrast see the facing page) but they were handled with great skill and a very sure taste. The interior above was designed by architect, Claudio Olivieri; and painter, Remo Muratore.

"Harmony and Proportion"

This display by Francesco Gnecchi-Ruscone is an exciting, sensitive presentation of a rather difficult and obscure subject commented on and shown in closer detail on page 97.

continued

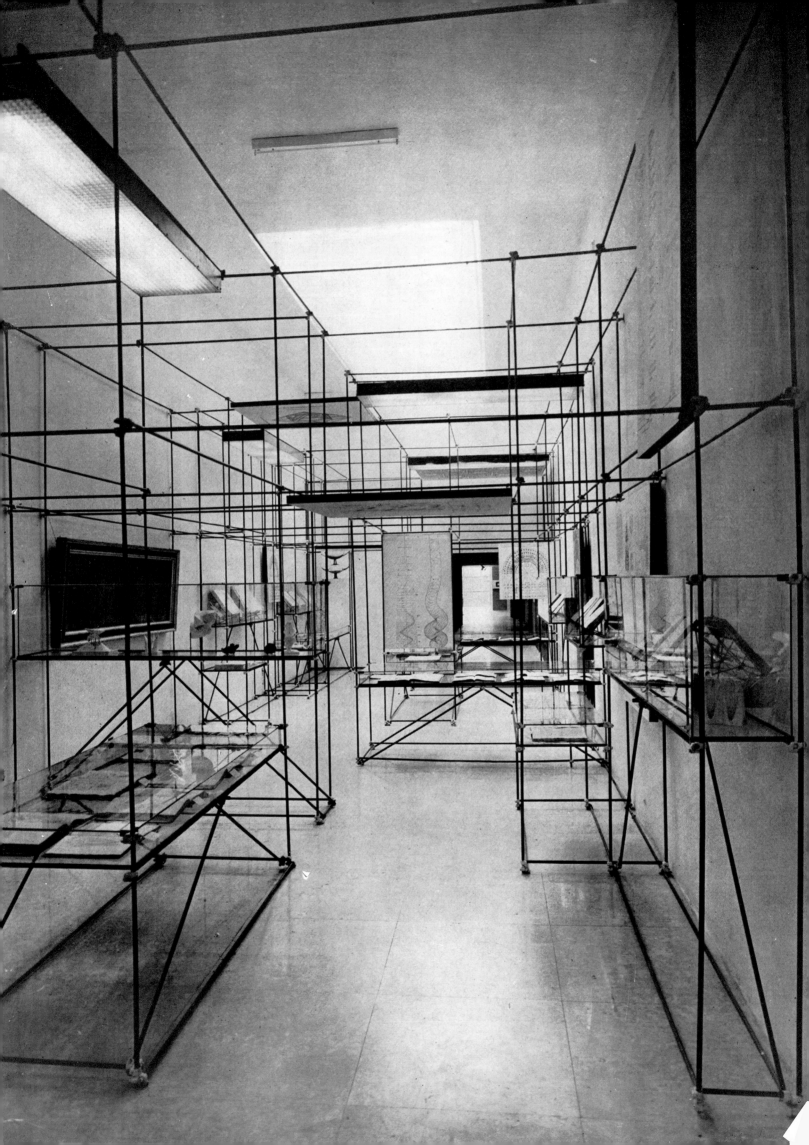

Architect Tapio Wirkkala filled Finland's section with the works of artists known the world over— with Ruth Byrk ceramics, Lisa Johansson-Pape lamps, Alvar Aalto furniture, Gunnel Nyman glass.

France presented city planning, painting, innumerable art objects (with glass and Lurcat tapestries outstanding) in spaces designed by architect Henry Prouvé with Charlotte Perriand.

West Germany's two floors, connected by Architect Max Wiederanders' winding stairs, showed objet d'art, factory items for interiors, photography and machines.

In Denmark's section, silver, porcelain, other handicrafts, several Finn Juhl and Hansen chairs stood on a platform of stretched canvas. Organizer was P. Wonsild; designer, Erik Herlow.

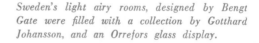

Sweden's light airy rooms, designed by Bengt Gate were filled with a collection by Gotthard Johansson, and an Orrefors glass display.

The Foreign Sections

Since the Triennale is an international show, there is always a section devoted to displays from other countries. Generally, as indicated by these photographs, the foreign exhibits are relatively small in size and modest in scope. At the 1951 exhibition the United States was the only country with a pavilion of its own. In a general way these foreign displays were revealing, though not in an unexpected way. The Scandinavian countries and Finland maintained, in both the products selected and the display designs themselves, a familiar, high standard of taste, with the handicrafts very much in evidence. The Swiss exhibit (page 76) showed the crisp clarity and superlative competence we have come to expect. France and Belgium had virtually nothing to contribute, a state of affairs which goes back to well before the war. Other countries, such as Germany and Austria, had spotty displays; partly because of the bad beating they took only a few years earlier, partly because designers had not yet gotten over the effects of officially dictated design policy from the Hitler regime. Generally speaking, the impression given at the Triennale was that Scandinavia and Switzerland were holding their own without much new evidence of progress; that France, Belgium, Spain and a few other countries were in a state of paralysis as far as creative design was concerned; and that Italy and this country were the only ones to show a real unfolding of ideas.

continued

The U. S. pavilion, as located in a grove of trees at the edge of a pond. This area was part of a park in which were also located the open-air transportation exhibit, the lookout tower and the café. The plan of the building consists of three non-concentric circles: the outer skin, an inner ring of structural poles, and a circular garden court.

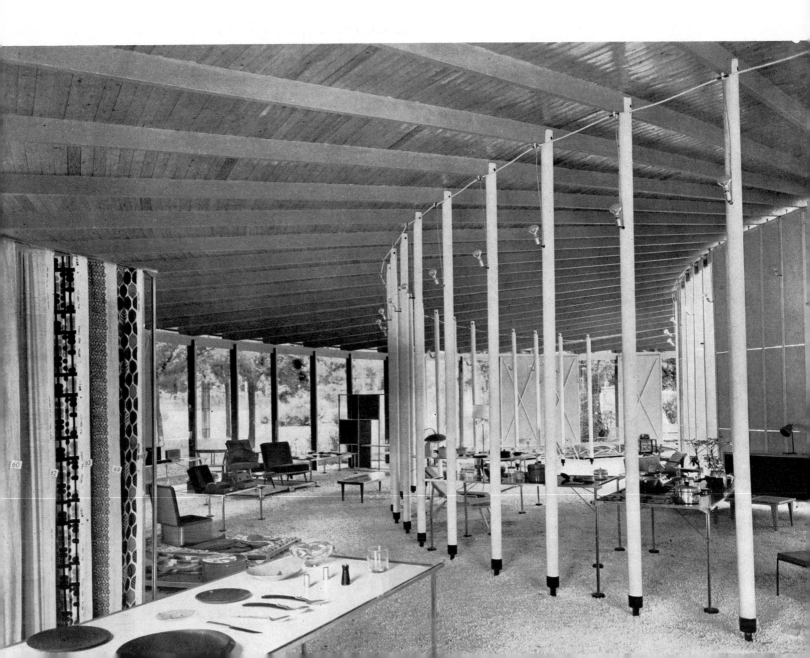

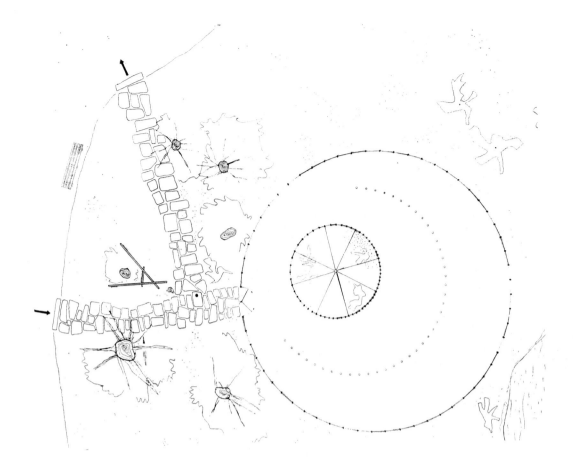

The United States Pavilion

It seems to be a persistent habit in most countries, where exhibits in international fairs are concerned, to deprecate one's own contribution. The British, for instance, who did a most creditable job on their own Festival of 1951, saw their own show at the Triennale as "a pathetic collection of photographs on battered cards with English captions," but considered the U. S. exhibit outstanding among the foreign displays. However, reactions to our exhibit in the U. S. were by no means quite so uniformly favorable. When one recalls that up to quite recently it was official opinion that the best way to represent U. S. life and culture was to ship out an undersized version of Mount Vernon. or something of the sort, our representation at the Triennale doesn't look quite so bad.

There are two main components in the U. S. show at Milan: the exhibits and the building. The exhibit was assembled by the Museum of Modern Art, and its contents are the same as those selected for the annual "Good Design" shows in Chicago and New York. It can therefore be judged on the same basis as the other material. The only important change from a display point of view is that the small objects here are arranged on knock-down tables of standard size, a scheme necessitated by the fact that the show was designed for traveling.

The building seems in every respect admirable. Its shape, and the pole supports strongly suggest a circus tent—a structure with which no critic has yet been able to find fault—and the dual suggestion of impermanence combined with elegance is, in these circumstances, entirely appropriate. The "floor" of the exhibit is gravel, a cheap solution and a good one. In structures of this type, where fragility is indicated both by the short period of use and the budget, it is always the details which count, and in the U. S. pavilion the details are both interesting and impeccable. The poles which socket so neatly into their metal bases and split to grasp the rafters; the indirect lighting consisting of reflector lamps on the poles, with wiring completely in the open; the skin, made up of panels of glass and plywood, with exposed bracing where its use is indicated—all of these add up to a successful, distinguished piece of display architecture. Credit to the U. S. is due chiefly for the excellent judgement in selecting the architects who happen to be one of the best firms practicing in Italy today: Belgiojoso, Peressutti and Rogers.

continued

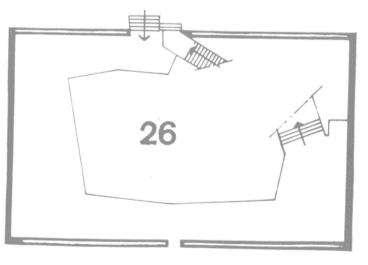

"The Italian Chair Through the Ages"

The job of doing an exhibit devoted to the various forms taken by chairs through the ages is not the easiest one which might be handed to a designer. The fact that the objects themselves are all roughly the same in size and scale and their disassociation from surroundings in which they are customarily seen, present difficulties which are close to being insurmountable. One possible approach would be to suggest relationships with backgrounds, and one of the most interesting things about the exhibit at the Triennale is the complete firmness with which this apparently easy way out was rejected. There is nothing in this display but the objects. Even the aid of color was put aside. The use of stages at different levels was the device adopted to create the illusion of movement and variety, and standard platforms were introduced to call attention to the chairs and to give a sense of unity through repetition. *continued*
Designer: Ignazio Gardella.

XIX   XIX   XIX   XIX

The Gallery of Glass is a long, elegant and not particularly "Italian" passageway, set above the arcade of a restaurant and used for display as well as communication. What is characteristic about the design is not so much the interior, which might as easily have originated in Switzerland or Scandinavia, but the view which appears in the small photograph at the top of the page. As inheritors of a tradition in art and architecture so old and so rich that the existence of masterpieces on every street corner is taken for granted by every child, the Italians have never treated their architectural patrimony with the exaggerated reverence one finds in other countries. The glass corridor is a good example. The original building was done in the arched masonry style considered "modern" before the war, and the glass passage makes no concessions to it, either in scale or style. This complete lack of interest in making things "match" does much to explain the fresh liveliness of so much Italian design.

The scheme of the corridor is simplicity itself. The inner wall consists of a series of alcoves created by vertical fins and glass shelves. The exhibits are toplighted and backlighted, a scheme which works well for glass in its transparent forms. On the open side there is no display wall, but the structural columns serve double duty as shelf supports and lighting standards. Here the display consists of ceramics which look well in silhouette against the glass wall. The interior is predominantly white, and the full-length skylight is a decisive element in a scheme whose main characteristics are luminosity and elegance. Architect: Roberto Menghi. Display designers: Elio Palazzo and Gian Luigi Reggi.

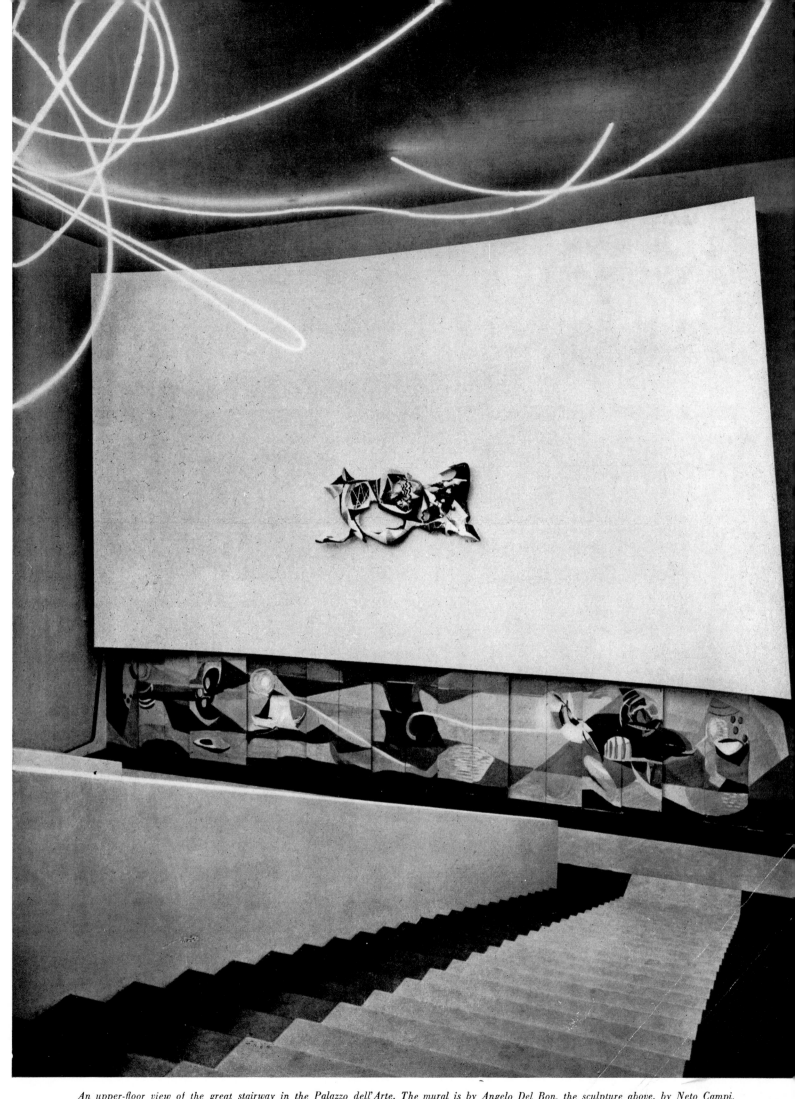

An upper-floor view of the great stairway in the Palazzo dell'Arte. The mural is by Angelo Del Bon, the sculpture above, by Neto Campi.

manufacturers of standard systems

H-System: 24, 25

Martin Metal & Associates
221 Bridgeway
Sausalito, Calif.

Laboratory Frames: 36, 37
Castaloy Laboratory Appliances
Flexaframe

Fisher Scientific Company
635 Greenwich Street
New York 14, N. Y.

17 Forbes Street
Pittsburgh 19, Pa.

Apparatus Support Frames and Clamps

The Emil Greiner Company
22 N. Moore Street
New York 13, N. Y.

Seelingrill: 38

Bliss Display Corporation
460 West 34 Street
New York 1, N. Y.

Struc-Tube: 15, 16, 17, 18, 19, 20, 21, 22, 23

Affiliated Machine & Tool Company
260 West Street
New York 13, N. Y.

Unistrut: 12, 13, 14, 129, 147

Unistrut Products Company
1013 Washington Blvd.
Chicago 7, Ill.

architects and designers

index

research and layout: Suzanne Sekey

book jacket and cover: Irving Harper   George Nelson and Associates

Interiors Library trademark: George Tscherny

engravings: City Photo Engraving Corporation
printing: Barnes Printing Company
binding: J. F. Tapley Company